Research, Realpolitik, and Development in Korea

THE RURAL STUDIES SERIES
of the
Rural Sociological Society

Board of Editors
1987-1988

Frederick H. Buttel, *Cornell University* (Chair)
Charles C. Geisler, *Cornell University* (Associate Chair)

Eileen S. Stommes, *New York State Department
of Agriculture and Markets*
Theodore D. Fuller, *Virginia Polytechnic Institute and State University*
Forrest A. Deseran, *Louisiana State University*
Donald R. Field, *Oregon State University and National Park Service*

Rural Studies Series

Rural Public Services: International Comparisons, edited by Richard E. Lonsdale and György Enyedi
The Social Consequences and Challenges of New Agricultural Technologies, edited by Gigi M. Berardi and Charles C. Geisler
†*Rural Society in the U.S.: Issues for the 1980s,* edited by Don A. Dillman and Daryl J. Hobbs
Technology and Social Change in Rural Areas: A Festschrift for Eugene A. Wilkening, edited by Gene F. Summers
†*Science, Agriculture, and the Politics of Research,* Lawrence Busch and William B. Lacy
†*The Cooperative Extension Service: A National Assessment,* Paul D. Warner and James A. Christenson
The Organization of Work in Rural and Urban Labor Markets, Patrick M. Horan and Charles M. Tolbert II
The Impact of Population Change on Business Activity in Rural America, Kenneth M. Johnson
Small Farms: Persistence with Legitimation, Alessandro Bonanno
Studies in the Transformation of U.S. Agriculture, edited by Eugene Havens with Gregory Hooks, Patrick H. Mooney, and Max J. Pfeffer
Family Farming in Europe and America, edited by Boguslaw Galeski and Eugene Wilkening
Electric Power for Rural Growth: How Electricity Affects Rural Life in Developing Countries, Douglas F. Barnes
The Rural South in Crisis: Challenges for the Future, edited by Lionel J. Beaulieu

†Available in hardcover and paperback.

Research, Realpolitik, and Development in Korea

The State and the Green Revolution

Larry L. Burmeister

Westview Press / Boulder and London

Rural Studies Series, Sponsored by the Rural Sociological Society

This Westview softcover edition is printed on acid-free paper and bound in softcovers that carry the highest rating of the National Association of State Textbook Administrators, in consultation with the Association of American Publishers and the Book Manufacturers' Institute.

All rights reserved. No part of this publication may be reproduced or transmitted in any form or by any means, electronic or mechanical, including photocopy, recording, or any information storage and retrieval system, without permission in writing from the publisher.

Copyright © 1988 by the Rural Sociological Society

Published in 1988 in the United States of America by Westview Press, Inc.; Frederick A. Praeger, Publisher; 5500 Central Avenue, Boulder, Colorado 80301

Library of Congress Cataloging-in-Publication Data
Burmeister, Larry L.
  Research, realpolitik, and development in Korea.
  (Rural studies series)
  Includes index.
  Bibliography: p.
  1. Agriculture—Research—Korea (South)
  2. Agriculture and state—Korea (South) 3. Green Revolution—Korea (South) I. Title. II. Series: Rural studies series of the Rural Sociological Society.
  S542.K8B87 1988   338.1'8519'5   87-12828
  ISBN 0-8133-7400-6

Printed and bound in the United States of America

∞   The paper used in this publication meets the requirements of the American National Standard for Permanence of Paper for Printed Library Materials Z39.48-1984.

6 5 4 3 2 1

Contents

List of Tables, ix
Acknowledgments, xi
Abbreviations, xiii

1. Introduction—Bringing Agriculture Back In: Agricultural Research and Korea's "Economic Miracle," 1
   Overview of the Book, 8

2. The State, Latecomer Industrialization, and Agricultural Research, 12
   Latecomer Industrialization and State Intervention, 12
   The State and Agricultural Research, 17
   The Politics of Agricultural Research, 18
   Induced or Directed Innovation? Implications for Development Theory, 26

3. State and Society in Korea: Sociopolitical Context of Public Sector Investment in Agricultural Research, 30
   The International Nexus of Contemporary Korean Politics, 31
   The State and the Countryside in Colonial Korea, 32
   The American Military Government in Korea, 35
   Postindependence Political Consolidation, 38
   The Social Landscape of the Countryside, 44
   Historical Continuities in Statist Domination? 47

4. Korea's Green Revolution: Rice Research as State Development Policy, 50
   The Development and Diffusion of an Improved Rice Variety, 50
   The Farmer's Role in Varietal Development and Diffusion, 55
   The Rise and Fall of Tongil, 60
   The Korean Green Revolution and the Developmental State, 65

5. Research Priorities: State Power or Market Power? 75
   *Korean Agricultural Research Budget Allocations
   in Comparative Perspective,* 75
   Korean Agricultural Research System Outputs, 87
   *The Visible Hand of the State in Agricultural
   Research Resource Allocation,* 92

6. Scientist Decision Making Within the Office of Rural
   Development: Authority and Influence Patterns, 98
   Research Decisions: Whose Preferences Count? 99
   ORD Organizational Structure, 104
   *Administrative Authority and ORD Scientist
   Behavior,* 106
   Clientele Influence and ORD Scientist Behavior, 111
   Scientific Influence and ORD Scientist Behavior, 117
   *Summing Up: Authority, Influence, and the ORD
   Division of Labor,* 122
   Hard State, Flexible Response? 127
   Appendix 6-A: Survey Questionnaire, 134
   Appendix 6-B: Key Informant Interviews, 146

7. Agricultural Research Policy in the NICs:
   Korea in Comparative Perspective, 150
   The Taiwanese Comparison, 152
   The Latin American Comparison, 156
   Patterns of State Intervention and Societal Response, 162
   *From Agricultural Research Policy to World System
   Theory,* 165

   References, 174
   Subject Index, 188
   Author Index, 196

List of Tables

1-1. Korean Socioeconomic Indicators, 2
4-1. Rice Variety and Production Data (1970-1983), 61
4-2. Diffusion Patterns of Tongil and Tongil-type Varieties (1976-1978), 62
4-3. Rice Prices (1962-1979), 67
4-4. Marketing of Rice Through Government Channels (1970-1983), 68
5-1. Cross-National Comparison of Research-Commodity Congruity Indices, 78
5-2. Korean Research-Commodity Congruity Index, 81
5-3. Research Commodity Percentage Breakdowns, 82
5-4. Research Expenditures as a Percentage of the Value of Production for Selected Commodities (1972-1979), 83
5-5. Korean Research Intensities (1962-1984), 84
5-6. Trends in Food Commodity Demand in Korea, 85
5-7. Agricultural Production Trends: Crop Acreage and Livestock Inventory (1962-1980), 86
5-8. Number of ORD Released Varieties (1963-1980), 88
5-9. Number of Korean Research Publications by Commodity Group (1963-1979), 91
6-1. Administrative Authority Indicators, 108-110
6-2. Clientele Influence Indicators, 113-115
6-3. Scientific Influence Indicators, 119-120
6-4. ORD Scientist Communication Patterns, 124-125
6-5. Scientific Cooperation Indicators, 126

Acknowledgments

During the course of graduate studies at Cornell University, Gene Erickson, Frank Young, and Randy Barker supplied much appreciated counsel and encouragement throughout the research process. Vernon Ruttan and Robert Evenson provided opportunities at crucial points in the development of the argument for discussions of their work and its implications for my project. Fred Buttel and Chuck Geisler gave much needed assistance during the manuscript review process in their roles as editors of the Rural Studies Series of the Rural Sociological Society. Two anonymous reviewers provided helpful suggestions for revisions. The intellectual influences of other scholars are acknowledged throughout the text. Unfortunately, none of the above can be blamed for my errors of interpretation and omission.

Field research support was provided by the East-West Center (EWC) under their Joint Doctoral Dissertation Intern program and a supplementary field research support grant was received from the International Agricultural Program at Cornell University. Bruce Koppel of the EWC's Resource Systems Institute was most considerate in arranging for an additional two months stay in Korea and in providing the most precious resource a scholar can command upon return from the field—an uninterrupted period for analysis and writing. A subsequent research visit supported by the Fulbright program in Korea offered an additional opportunity to update information and revisit interpretations.

At the University of Kentucky, editorial assistance has been graciously provided by Ann Stockham, Nancy Strang, and Mitsie Sample.

Only a few of us are accorded the privilege of living and studying in another society for an extended period of time. It is impossible to reciprocate the collective kindness and good-natured curiosity that such sojourns bring forth. I must list a few special Korean friends—Professor Shim Young-Kun and his family graciously received me upon my arrival in Korea and were most helpful throughout my stay; Professors Ban Sung-Hwan and Lee Jil-Hyun of the Seoul National University, College of Agriculture provided much needed assistance; graduate students Lee Kyong-Hoon and Chung Hee-Doo were caring friends and able research assistants. Other friends too numerous to mention responded to my trials and tribulations with patience and good humor. Many administrative officials and scientists at the Office of Rural Development helped with data collection and provided information about their research programs. I express my gratitude to numerous others—academicians, government officials, and farmers—who generously put aside what they were doing to talk with me about agricultural policy issues in Korea. The questions I asked were often politically sensitive. Even when put on an uncomfortable spot, responses were always gracious and my sometimes untoward interrogative manner was forgiven.

Finally, I dedicate this book to my parents—Ellen and Louis Burmeister. Their encouragement throughout an extended period of study and research has been a constant source of strength.

Larry L. Burmeister

Permission to use portions of the published materials listed below is acknowledged with appreciation. Chapters in the monograph in which this material appears are placed in parentheses following the citations.

> Larry L. Burmeister, "The South Korean Green Revolution: Induced or Directed Innovation?" *Economic Development and Cultural Change* 35:767-790 (portions of Chapter 4).
> Copyright, 1987, The University of Chicago Press.
> 0013/0079/87/3504-0048$01.00
>
> M. Ann Judd, James K. Boyce, and Robert E. Evenson, "Investing in Agricultural Supply: The Determinants of Agricultural Research and Extension Investment." *Economic Development and Cultural Change*, 34:77-113 (modified version of Table 6, p. 92 appears as Table 5-4).
> Copyright, 1986, The University of Chicago Press.
> 0013/0079/87/3501-0005$01.00

Abbreviations

AMG	American military government
BA	bureaucratic-authoritarian
BAIR	bureaucratic-authoritarian industrializing regime
CABA	*Commonwealth Agricultural Bureau Abstracts*
COMECON	Council of Mutual Economic Assistance
CORD	Central Office of Rural Development
DG	Director General (of ORD)
DMZ	demilitarized zone
EPB	Economic Planning Board
FA	farmers' association (Taiwan)
GDP	gross domestic product
IRRI	International Rice Research Institute
ISI	import substitution industrialization
JCRR	Joint Committee on Rural Reconstruction (Taiwan)
KASS	Korean Agricultural Sector Study
KMT	Kuomintang (Taiwan)
KPR	Korean People's Republic
MAF	Ministry of Agriculture and Fisheries (formerly, Forestry)
MCI	Ministry of Commerce and Industry
MHA	Ministry of Home Affairs
MITI	Ministry of International Trade and Industry (Japan)
MOF	Ministry of Finance (Japan)
NACF	National Agricultural Cooperatives Federation
NATO	North Atlantic Treaty Organization
NCM	New Community Movement (*Saemaul Undong*)
NIC	newly industrializing country
NKWP	North Korean Workers' Party
OECD	Organization for Economic Cooperation and Development
ORD	Office of Rural Development
PL 480	Public Law 480
PORD	Provincial Office of Rural Development
RGO	Rural Guidance Office
ROK	Republic of Korea
TNC	transnational corporation
USAID	United States Agency for International Development

1
INTRODUCTION
Bringing Agriculture Back In: Agricultural Research and Korea's "Economic Miracle"

The Republic of Korea's (hereafter Korea) rapid industrial growth is the focal point of most analyses of the country's stellar economic performance during the 1960s and 1970s. The recent growth rates of the manufacturing sector (see Table 1-1) have overwhelmed the steady, historically respectable growth rates that have occurred in agriculture (Hayami, Ruttan, and Southworth 1979; Krishna 1982). Agricultural sector contributions tend to be overlooked when industrial transformation occurs as rapidly as it has in Korea. In perhaps the most comprehensive recent overview of Korean rural development to appear in English, agricultural sector growth is treated primarily as a "demand pull" phenomenon. The authors of this volume conclude:

> Rural Korea's role in overall development . . . differs markedly from that of many other developing countries. A Korean agricultural revolution did not precede or lead development in the other sectors of the economy. There were no substantial net flows of savings and tax dollars from the rural to the urban sector. There was a flow of agricultural produce in exchange for manufactures, and, most important, a massive migration of labor from the farms into the factories, transport, and trade. For the most part, however, it was agriculture that benefitted from the industrial and export boom rather than the reverse. This boom provided a rapidly expanding market for farm output and for

TABLE 1-1. Korean Socioeconomic Indicators

Indicator	Unit	1960	1965	1970	1975	1980	1984
1. Total GNP[a]	billion won	7,541	10,211	17,284	26,113	37,205	49,180
2. Total population	1,000 persons	24,954	28,327	31,435	34,679	37,407	40,578
3. GNP per capita[a]	1,000 won	302	360	550	753	995	1,212
4. Agricultural GNP	% total	42.2	43.0	28.7	24.2	14.4	15.1
5. Rural population	% total	--	55.1	44.7	37.5	22.2	20.8
6. Agr. labor force	% total	66.4	59.6	51.6	46.4	32.3	25.9
7. Average farm size	ha	--	.91	.93	.94	1.02	1.09
8. Farm household income/urban household income	%	--	138	91	118	84	97

Growth rates:		1965-73	1973-84
9. Total GNP	%	10.0	7.2
10. Manufacturing GNP	%	21.1	11.5
11. Agricultural GNP	%	2.9	1.7

[a]Constant 1980 prices.

Sources: Bank of Korea (1986, Indicators 1-7); Park (1986: III-17); World Bank (1986, Indicators 9-11).

rural "surplus" labor, together with an increasing supply of such key inputs as chemical fertilizer and farm machinery. (Ban, Moon, and Perkins 1980:5)

This "minimalist" view of agriculture's role in development in Korea is pronounced in recent policy analyses which attempt to draw lessons from the Korean experience. For example, the most recent World Bank study of Korea makes only fleeting reference to agriculture in spite of the fact that over a quarter of the country's workforce is still employed in that sector (Leipziger 1987). The fact is that Korean agricultural sector policies do not fit the Bank's recent market-based, export-oriented growth prescriptions. The policy counsel the Bank extracts from the Korean story has been simplified into a "market rational" axiom—that is, the imperative of realigning domestic prices with international prices, with a realistic foreign exchange rate the key parameter (Krueger 1983). As Wood (1986) notes, the "state capitalist" dimensions of the Korean political economy are conveniently forgotten due to the Bank's current aversion to development alternatives that emphasize state intervention. Agriculture is thus selectively omitted from analyses that stress the importance of "getting the prices right."[1]

In fact, Korean policymakers have pursued a strategy of selective engagement in international markets. The realignment of some prices in selected export markets to effect *competitive* advantage in certain industrial activities has occurred in tandem with ubiquitous state intervention in pricing and marketing in other sectors to create strategic import substitution capabilities and domestic market linkages. What Korea represents is not an export industrializing regime based on undiluted principles of economic liberalism, but rather a state-orchestrated combination of import substitution and export industrialization (Luedde-Neurath 1986). Agricultural policies must be viewed as part of the import substitution component. In the 1970s, internal demand for domestically produced industrial products was created, and scarce foreign exchange was freed for the purchase of imports of intermediate and capital goods through state intervention in agriculture. The state deliberately "distorted" some markets in order to make the growing Korean industrial plant competitive on a world scale.[2]

Agricultural commodity prices in the Northeast Asian region (particularly the price of rice, the major foodgrain staple) are considerably higher than world market prices. A growing literature on the "political economy of agricultural protection" suggests that these policies reflect organized interest group pressures for guaranteed income streams. The shrinking impact of agricultural products in total consumption expenditures; the ability of smaller, more tightly organized groups of farmers to make common political cause (the Olson [1965] collective action argument); and the intractability of rural poverty in the midst of an increasingly affluent industrial society are adduced to have fostered an increasing degree of agricultural protectionism in Northeast Asia reminiscent of the Common Agricultural Policy in Europe (Anderson 1983). Organized interest groups are able to impose the "dead weight" economic efficiency losses of subsidized producer prices on society at large (Timmer 1986:146-147). In Korea, however, different social forces have been responsible for protectionist agricultural policies promulgated rather early in the industrialization process. Beginning in the late 1960s, state agents set higher prices for agricultural commodities to bring agricultural producers into national markets in a way that supported—economically and politically—the national industrialization project.[3] Agricultural commodity price policy was one instrument employed by state agents to influence the economic activities of farmers in a direction consonant with national production goals, rather than the outcome of society-centered political initiatives to secure private sector advantage.

In order to correct misleading interpretations about the role of Korean agriculture in the development process, a revised interpretation of the agricultural contributions to Korean industrial development is in order. Krishna's (1982) analysis of the recent economic history of the newly industrializing countries (NICs) emphasizes the complementary, interactive dynamics of mutually reinforcing agricultural sector and industrial sector growth.[4] Scitovsky (1985) and Hamilton (1986), from quite different theoretical perspectives, cite the important contributions of agriculture to Korean economic development. This linkage is not unexpected. In the course of the industrialization process, a surplus must be extracted from agriculture to support nascent industry. In the Korean case, too, "unproductive" resources have been transferred out of agriculture and into the factories; simultaneously, land and labor productivities in agriculture have increased at respectable rates

(Ban 1985).

The economic dynamism of Northeast Asia has encouraged comparative studies of the transition from an agricultural to an industrial economy in the countries of the region. Oshima (1986) argues that, compared to Japan and Taiwan, commensurate capital flows were not extracted from agriculture in Korea. Korean agriculture was thus comparatively "underdeveloped." Again, this reading of the agricultural contribution in Korea is misleading. During the decade following the Korean War, Korean policymakers maintained a low-price regime for staple foodgrains and low levels of infrastructural investment in agriculture. During the regime of President Rhee, both economic policy neglect and a concomitant aid maximization strategy were responsible. Subsequently, General-turned-President Park was preoccupied early in his tenure with economic stabilization problems which mitigated against higher agricultural price policies and increased public sector investment in agriculture. Yet this deliberate squeeze of agriculture, along with later agricultural sector stimulation policies, mobilized agricultural contributions to industrialization in indirect ways often difficult to measure—for example, first through the provision of cheap wage goods and the creation of economic incentives for the migration of educated rural youth to urban areas (with postprimary education expenses paid by rural households), and, later through the design of strategic consumption and industrialization linkages. In other words, there was a good deal of manipulated "supply response" in the agricultural sector. As a result, the narrow "demand pull" interpretation of Korean agricultural growth is an insufficient explanation of the dynamics of intersectoral linkage.

The linkage of Korean agriculture to the industrialization project remains underexplored. This author has argued that agriculture is, perhaps, the most tightly controlled sector of the Korean economy (Burmeister 1987b). Product prices, input subsidies, technology improvement campaigns, and state marketing channels have been used in tandem to encourage the articulation of agriculture and industry. National markets were created for agricultural products and inputs. A flow of wage goods and workers was provided to industry; protected domestic input markets in agriculture provided the necessary intersectoral linkages for industrialization pushes in the petrochemical and machinery sectors. An integrated agricultural policy package was promulgated by state agents to support the national industrialization project in the face of inevitable internal and external constraints (both political and economic).

In this study, agricultural research (and extension) policy is used to explore state mobilization of the countryside in support of agricultural development goals.[5] Why look closely at agricultural research policy? On the surface, agricultural research seems rather impervious to top-down mobilization dictates. The location specificity of agriculture implies decentralized strategies of technology development, adjustment, and diffusion. Success, in terms of adoption of improved technologies, is predicated on a modicum of local level cooperation. In addition, a cadre of scientists and technicians is located in a strategic organizational control position in the technology development, evaluation, and diffusion processes. The operational mode is one of systematic monitoring of environmental feedback to assure a close fit between technical change and on-the-farm practice. The optimal change path is one of gradual adjustment, rather than rapid mobilization. Because the Korean experience contradicts conventional notions about the agricultural research process, an in-depth study of agricultural research activities promises to reveal in stark terms how agriculture has been mobilized in support of Korean economic development.

Another important reason for focusing on agricultural research policies is that this issue has been well integrated into the development literature in the social sciences. The induced innovation model (Hayami and Ruttan 1985; Binswanger and Ruttan 1978) has played a seminal role in providing an endogenous "political economy" explanation of agricultural research initiatives.[6] That is, attention has been directed to the political processes through which the public goods (such as agricultural research) necessary for economic growth are provided. Technology generation has been conceptualized as a social process rather than treated as an exogenous variable in explanations of development.

Moreover, the heuristic impact of the induced innovation model is shown by subsequent revisions and/or critiques of induced innovation contributions. The original proponents have reflected on past work by extending the scope of previous analyses and clarifying previous positions (Ruttan 1981, 1982, 1983). Critics of the model have reworked induced innovation ideas in ways that provide further insights into the social determinants of technical change paths, often incorporating seminal induced innovation ideas into quite different theoretical paradigms of socioeconomic change (de Janvry 1978, 1981; Grabowski 1982; de Janvry and Dethier 1985; Piniero and Trigo 1983). These spin-offs have helped anchor the agricultural research issue in the broader context of debates in development theory. Thus, the discussion of the Korean agricultural research experience can be situated in a body of literature directly linking the technical change process to social structural variables, especially the state/society relationship.

This last point is crucial because agricultural research programs are often sponsored and funded by the state. In the development literature, variation in state economic intervention proclivities, along with the effectiveness of different intervention strategies, have become focal points of attention (Evans, Rueschemeyer, and Skocpol 1985; Evans, Rueschemeyer, and Stephans 1985; Katzenstein 1985). Many analysts argue that Korean development has been state-directed (Hamilton 1986; Luedde-Neurath 1986; Burmeister 1986; Wade and White 1984; Haggard and Moon 1983; Jones and Sakong 1980). As yet, state intervention in Korean agriculture has not received due consideration.

The title of this monograph summarizes the argument put forth. In Korea, development—*defined substantively* (not normatively) *as competitive industrialization*—has been spurred by state intervention to accelerate capital accumulation. A wide array of goods and services necessary to prime the industrial pump, including agricultural research, has been provided under state auspices. State agents were acting to advance a national development project within a world system of isomorphic (but vastly unequal) nation-state units. In this highly competitive international arena, realpolitik objectives drove policy—that is, state officials promulgated economic development initiatives to advance the relative position of their unit vis-à-vis competing national units (List 1844). Colonial experience (Myers and Saburo 1984; Cumings 1984b), geopolitical conflict (Kihl 1984), and political culture (Pye 1985) combined to reinforce the potential capacity of the Korean state to intervene ubiquitously in the economy in the guise of a national development imperative. In light of the increasing state-centeredness of development theory, it is felt that analysis of the Korean agricultural research experience will enhance knowledge of the types of state/society relationships that undergird NIC incorporation into and advance within the world political economy.

The relationship between the state and society in Korea is changing as this monograph is being written. In the future, state agents will be more constrained by societal forces than they were during the period reviewed in this study (Burmeister 1987c). However, future policies will be formulated in response to legacies of state intervention. Contrary to the hopes of policymakers who decry agricultural sector inefficiency, benign neglect of agriculture is not a feasible policy option.[7] The economic geography of industrial growth in Korea has left many regions of the country still dominated by the agricultural economy, with bleak prospects for increases in off-farm income earning opportunities in the short run (Ho 1982). Regional political tensions have been heightened by increased regional economic disparities. Thus it is difficult to see how aggressive agricultural policy measures designed to force sectoral accommodation to international efficiency benchmarks (e.g., world market prices and increased economies of size in farming) in the staple foodgrain sector (rice and barley) are politically possible, at least in the medium term. The preface of any workable political liberalization scheme is the availability of economic resources at the provincial and local levels which can be tapped by autonomous governing units. A serious, precipitous decline in the agricultural economy would make the political transition even more problematic than it appears at present. Understanding past agricultural development initiatives is a prerequisite for dealing effectively with Korea's current agricultural adjustment problems.

Overview of the Book

In Chapter 2, a generic argument outlining the relationship between latecomer industrialization, state intervention, and agricultural research policy is presented. Latecomer industrialization is associated with state power aggrandizement at the expense of societal (class, interest group) power. As a consequence, agricultural research policies often reflect state preferences rather than aggregated individual or group preferences based on position in the market. This argument is advanced by a critique of the induced innovation theory of technical/institutional change which emphasizes market forces in explanations of agricultural research policy dynamics. A brief review of the growth of public sector agricultural research capacity in the United States and Japan, exemplary case studies in the induced innovation literature, is presented to illustrate the need to consider extra-market determinants of agricultural research and extension institutionalization and policy direction.

Chapter 3 chronicles the emergence of a statist mode of social domination in postindependence Korea. Major themes emphasized are the exclusionary politics of the Korean developmental state, the commitment of state agents to rapid industrialization within the world political economy, and the relations between the state and the countryside that facilitated an intersectoral transfer of resources as Korea shifted from an agrarian to an industrial society.

The Korean green revolution is the subject of Chapter 4. Technical change is conceptualized as state-initiated directed innovation. Evidence is adduced at the processual level—that is, how agricultural research and extension decisions were made and implemented at key points in the research, adaptation, and dissemination cycles in the high-yield rice variety development campaign that was the foundation of the Korean green revolution.

In Chapter 5, the argument about the relative weight of state and societal preferences in agricultural research decision making is scrutinized further through an analysis of how budgetary resources and personnel were allocated to different agricultural research activities. Emphasis is placed on the commodity orientation of the agricultural research program and its lack of correspondence with demand and supply trends in an increasingly market-oriented agriculture.

Chapter 6 moves to questions about communication patterns, work activities, and perceived social influences on research among agricultural scientists within Korea's agricultural research system. The relative weight of three important social influences on research activities—administrative, scientific, and clientele—are analyzed to gauge research organization response within the context of the Korean state/society relationship.

Chapter 7 concludes the discussion by putting the Korean agricultural research experience in comparative perspective. Attention will be focused on other NICs with "exclusionary" political regime types—Taiwan and several Latin American countries—to assess how differences in state/society relationships affect agricultural research system priorities. The impact of these priorities on national industrialization experiences is briefly considered.

Notes

1. Reading between the lines, a benign scenario is a gradual phaseout of "inefficient" agricultural activities. It is hoped that demographics, the continuing migration of rural youth to the cities and the aging of the economically active farm population, will eliminate the agricultural policy problem in the years ahead. The rural sector's dependence on the central government for a wide array of agricultural services was easily manipulated to assure rural sector support for the government party in periodic elections and plebisicites. Demographic trends have mitigated the effective weight of the rural electorate, thus making it easier in theory to dismantle gradually what many policymakers regard as suboptimal agricultural policies, particularly foodgrain price supports and input subsidies.

2. Zysman (1983) assesses the role of market "distortions" in achieving competitive advantage in strategic international markets. He makes an important distinction between competitive and comparative advantage in international trade which describes the dynamics of Korea's selective engagement in international markets.

3. Discussions of state intervention in pricing and marketing can be found in Ban, Moon, and Perkins (1980); Kihl (1979); Kihl and Bark (1981); Kim and Joo (1982); and Moon (1975).

4. The term newly industrializing countries (NICs) is applied to a set of third world countries that have shown similar patterns of sustained aggregate economic growth, increased industrialization, and export market penetration in manufactured goods during the 1960s and 1970s. An OECD study (1979) grouped South Korea, Taiwan, Hong Kong, Singapore, Mexico, Brazil, Portugal, Greece, Yugoslavia, and Spain together as NICs. Many of the third world countries often included in the NIC category are classified together as "upper middle-income" countries in the *World Development Report 1986*. NICs are often referred to as semiperipheral countries in world system theory. For a theoretical discussion of the import of this classification, see Browett (1985).

5. The focus of this study is the public sector agricultural research system. Most of the data collected pertains to agricultural research decision making with scientists as the key informants and respondents. It is quite difficult, however, to

separate research and extension when discussing agricultural research policies and program implementation in Korea. Thus, during the course of this analysis, it has often been necessary to speak of conjoined research and extension initiatives as integrated policy responses.

6. To avoid confusion, it is necessary to define what is meant here by political economy. Following Gilpin (1987:9), political economy indicates a "set of questions" relating to the interactive and cyclical dynamics between politics and economics or, in social structural terms, relations between the state and the market. The term political economy is not used to connote a particular methodological or theoretical approach in the analysis of this interaction. In this argument, state-centered and society-centered models of public sector agricultural research activities are contrasted as alternative "political economy" models in the sense that different ideas about how the state, private actors, and market forces interact are used to explain particular agricultural research program trajectories. See Gilpin (1987, Ch. 1) for a statement which reflects rather closely the way the term political economy is used here.

7. The grain management and fertilizer funds set up to finance price supports and input subsidies are provided largely by overdrafts on the Bank of Korea. This inflationary method of program support came under increasing fire during the late 1970s, as inflation reached worrisome levels. The total accumulated deficit amassed from these funds during the period 1970-1982 was estimated at approximately two billion U.S. dollars (Moon 1984:68). In the 1980s, gradual reductions in the yearly increases in administered staple foodgrain prices and increases in the prices farmers pay for fertilizer have reduced the fiscal burden somewhat. Using the producer/consumer surplus method of social welfare accounting, Martin and McDonald (1986:324) calculated that the social loss due to agricultural price supports was equivalent to 1.09% of the total GNP in 1977. Such are the dimensions of economic inefficiency referred to in recent neoclassical partial equilibrium analyses of Korean agricultural policy.

2
The State, Latecomer Industrialization, and Agricultural Research

The pioneering works of Gerschenkron (1962) and Bendix (1967) recognized the link between the historical sequencing of industrialization and levels of state intervention in economic affairs. Bourgeois-liberal, mercantilist, state socialist, and now NIC patterns of industrialization represent adaptations to external circumstances as well as internal accommodations to group struggles for political and economic advantage. What this means for a theory of agricultural research activities (and development theory, in general) is explored in this chapter.

Latecomer Industrialization and State Intervention

Horowitz (1982) argues persuasively that development in the late twentieth century means industrialization. A competitive industrial base is required for nation-states to secure a viable niche in the world economy. Among the NICs, the industrial transformation is apt to be state-led. This is due to a combination of external competitive pressures and internal social circumstances.

The advent of the state as a primary "power container" (Giddens 1985) is due to the interstate dimension of the modern world system, creating an environment in which like social units (nation-states) coexist, compete, and measure relative "power-prestige" (Collins 1986). The interstate system is organized on principles of "self-help" (Waltz 1979). There is no overarching supranational authority that insures individual unit welfare or guarantees unit autonomy. Various internal societal mobilization mechanisms (e.g., taxation, conscription, indoctrination, surveillance) deployed to meet external challenges have been sanctioned reflexively by gradual recognition of principles of juridical and territorial sovereignty that define "stateness" in the world political economy (Ruggie 1983b). The characteristic authority position and resource bases of state agents that flow from societywide powers of institution-building and the monopoly of organized coercion have emerged as a result of interstate system dynamics.

The logic of the interstate system is revealed in the dual warfare/welfare imperative imposed systemically on all individual units (Burmeister 1986). Social welfare gains in "reference societies" are reflexively monitored across units. The stability of particular governing regimes (and regime types—i.e., institutional governing arrangements) within units depends in part on whether some semblance of parity in living standards and social development can be maintained or aspired to. In addition to the welfare imperative, state officials must worry about external threats to unit integrity. Military preparedness in an era of rapid technological change requires a substantial commitment of state resources. These dual warfare/welfare imperatives mean that the dominant classes in all but the most resource-poor ministates define development as industrialization. Industrialization promises to increase the amount of extractable resources at the disposal of state officials, thus increasing their ability to cope with the warfare/welfare problem.

The reflexive character of the modern world system creates chronic legitimation problems for third world elites. Social expectations run high in the late twentieth century. People see what is happening in other units and, as a consequence, become conscious of wide disparities in social well-being across national boundaries. The postwar superpower conflict with its attendant global militarization has provided the physical means for internal social control via the transfer of material and organizational means of coercion monopolized by the state. Brute force, however, often provides only temporary relief from pressures from below. Eventually, new social arrangements that increase production and consumption opportunities must be generated and nurtured in an effort to close the welfare gap.

The historical sequencing of industrialization is a crucial determinant of constraints and opportunities facing state officials who seek to upgrade the productive potential of their jurisdictions. Unfortunately for the upstarts, especially the so-called third world countries that obtained formal independence from the colonial powers in the post-World War II era, a development strategy is fashioned in a crowded arena of entrenched competitors. The industrial latecomers require capital, technology, and market access. The rules by which capital and technology are diffused and markets opened, however, were established by the earlier industrializers in response to their particular interests. The structural reality of the present "one world economy" (Feinberg 1983) is international oligopoly (Newfarmer 1983). There are opportunities for ascent within the world system, but these opportunities are bounded (Ruggie 1983c). New entrants must adapt to the prices, standards, and technical know-how set by the leading industrial powers.

Sociologically, initial industrialization pushes are social struggles to impose patterns of intersectoral articulation—that is, flows of transactions in goods and services (including labor) between agriculture and industry. The classical outline of this process in found in Polanyi (1957). An agrarian order based on the social logic of labor immobility and self-sufficiency is replaced by an industrial order based on labor mobility and economic interdependence. Social conflicts to impose intersectoral articulation within particular national confines pit coalitions of the landed aristocracy, the nascent bourgeoisie, state officials (including the military), and "popular classes" against each other (Moore 1966). The social composition of these struggles and their outcomes have been, of course, contingent on historically specific international and local circumstances. Earlier bourgeois-liberal modes of industrial transformation gave way to mercantile-statist modes at the turn of the century (Gerschenkron 1962; Bendix 1967). The Bolshevik Revolution produced an autarkic, revolutionary counter-response to previous capitalist industrial paths.

It is in response to this historical legacy that the current group of "late" latecomers—the NICS of the third world—learn and adapt. Like the second generation latecomers (Russia, Prussia, Italy, Japan), the relative power of the state over societal actors seems pronounced in those countries that are following the capitalist path. State officials, rather than private groups, have often taken the lead in mobilizing capital, labor, and technology in support of a rapid industrialization program. As Stepan notes (1978:xii), state officials have often restructured relationships within civil society, in effect creating an incipient social class structure supportive of industrialization. A complex set of world system, state, and class interactions has generated distinctive patterns of state/society accommodations in this fourth generation of latecomers (Koo 1984).[1]

The NICs, by and large, are following "associative" strategies designed to obtain resources from advanced capitalist countries and their transnational corporations (TNCs) (Ruggie 1983c). Postwar geopolitical ties with the United States have faciliated aid and trade in Taiwan and Korea. In Latin America, western capitalist economic penetration following formal independence in the nineteenth century resulted in strong ties between local elites and foreign economic interests. As attested by an emerging literature comparing "bureaucratic-authoritarian" regimes, these different types of "associative" experiences have fostered different social power structures resulting in different outcomes, both economic and political (Im 1987; Lim 1985; Collier 1979). It appears, however, that positional advance within the world system requires some type of international linkage, and these ties are more likely to be sought in the West. The economic stagnation of the state socialist economies leaves the "late" latecomers with few promising linkage options. The socialist camp is also now dependent on its capitalist competitors for new technology to stave off economic stagnation (Goldman 1983). The limits of socialist autarky have become strikingly apparent following China's policy reversal toward a more open economy during the late 1970s.

This lack of options presents serious difficulties for the NICs. Advanced capitalist countries and their TNCs drive hard bargains. In order for the NICs to maximize returns from economic exchanges that procure capital, technology, and market access, a negotiating authority is required that can, on occasion, dictate the conditions of national procurement and use. Private interests cannot be trusted to balance the diverse industrial deepening, sectoral articulation, and employment goals of state policymakers seeking competitive international and viable domestic economic development outcomes. State officials have the authority to take the lead. State controls over capital and labor provide some leverage over how international linkages are managed.

Latecomer industrialization engenders the "developmental state," even under capitalist modes of socioeconomic organization. A state/society relationship emerges in which state capacity for direct economic intervention is unusually high by bourgeois-liberal standards (Evans and Rueschemeyer 1985). This capacity is exercised not for ideological reasons, as in "state socialist" societies, but to mobilize resources for industrialization. According to Johnson (1982, Ch. 1), economic policy in the developmental state focuses on substantive goals and targets related to competition (both economic and politicomilitary) among nations. Policy interventions are "plan rational." This is in contrast to the bourgeois-liberal mode of "market rational" policy interventions designed to spur economic efficiency through adjustment of the rules and procedures governing competition between private economic actors. These different industrial policies reflect differences in the relative social power of state officials and private interests.

The autonomy of the developmental state is lodged in key organizational parameters—centralization of the policymaking apparatus, social isolation of the bureaucracy, corporatist control of interest groups, etc. (Katzenstein 1978). The structural realities of the modern world system have engendered patterns of social domination in the developmental state mold in several of the NICs, with Korea and Taiwan being exemplars. The structural reasons for state power aggrandizement are fourfold. First, an expansive state apparatus was imposed on "peripheral" societies during colonial rule (Alavi 1972). This apparatus proved to be a primary power resource in the postindependence struggles for political control; thus it was often left intact. Second, economic competition on a world scale requires entrepreneurial capabilities that nascent capitalists are unable or unwilling to provide. State officials step in to initiate and manage infrastructural investments and strategic industries. Third, state officials are in a position to play this economic role because the state as an organization is accorded fiscal and planning authority that is respected by other states and international agencies (Meyer 1981). Through this authority, the fiscal and legal means to initiate and nurture a national industrialization project are summoned. Finally, the "globalization" of the superpower conflict has fostered a developmental response (Horowitz 1982).

The impact of world military conflict on state capacity/autonomy requires further amplification. The postwar bipolar politicomilitary conflict has resulted in a nuclear stalemate. The threat of nuclear annihilation has made direct military conflict between the United States and the Soviet Union problematic. As a result, this confrontation has been displaced to third world turf. The military sector of the third world state apparatus has received substantial flows of resources from the superpowers—not only military hardware, but "software" such as overseas technical training and organizational skills. These resources have placed the military in a strategic position both within the state apparatus and vis-à-vis weaker and less organized civilian groups. Internal class structures are not crystallized to the extent found in the early industrializers. This situation confers significant political, economic, and sociological advantages on the military as catalysts of national development efforts. In politics the nationalist cloak fits well; exposure to the benefits of high technology provides economic direction; and sociologically, the ideologies of efficiency and austerity are emphasized and extolled (Horowitz 1982:96-106). In addition, the military often "enjoys" a degree of social insulation from other groups. This has made it somewhat easier for state officials in military-controlled regimes to promote and implement a national development project that may clash with particular societal interests.

The State and Agricultural Research

Historically, agricultural research and extension activities have often been sponsored and funded by the state in support of economic development goals. According to many scholars, state involvement occurs because of the "public goods'" characteristics of agricultural research that render these services "nonmarketable" (Steiner 1977:27-66). That is, agricultural research products often consist of information, which should be disseminated as rapidly as possible for maximum impact. The conventional market—a rationing mechanism that restricts goods and services to a clientele willing and able to pay—is often an unsuitable means of information dissemination. Other agricultural research products, such as self-pollinating seed varieties, are easily exchanged and propagated outside commercial channels. New cultural practices may be acquired merely through observation. Private incentives for the production of these goods and services, essential for agricultural productivity increases, are weak. The state must fill the void. A significant body of literature within both the neoclassical economic (Mueller 1979) and Neomarxist (O'Connor 1973) traditions explains this type of state intervention in the economy.

Technology generation is also a means of societal mobilization. Effective technologies increase production. The resulting surplus can be channeled into a variety of projects based on the decisions of those who control its disposition. Partial state control of the surplus is often effected through taxation, parastatal marketing, price controls, etc. Thus state sponsorship of agricultural research can be conceptualized in a more proactive fashion than is connoted by traditional "reactive" treatments—for example, emphasis on market imperfections (the neoclassical approach) or on attempts to meliorate accumulation crises (the Neomarxist approach). Research can be used by state officials to direct the social development path in ways consistent with a plan.

In either case, the provision of a portfolio of agricultural research activities is a political process. Important choices about commodity emphasis, factor bias (capital-saving or labor-saving innovations), and the targeted clientele (large commercial farmers, small subsistence-oriented farmers, urban consumers, etc.) must be made. These choices determine who gets what from the allocation of material and organizational resources committed to agricultural research. The research decision-making process tells us much about the relationship between state and society that defines a particular national development experience.

Simply put, the sociology of development is the analysis of the formation of historically specific state/society relationships within the crucible of worldwide industrial transformation. A chapter in this story is the emergence in the midnineteenth century of state-supported agricultural research to expand agricultural productivity to facilitate a greater flow of resources from agriculture to industry (Ruttan 1982, Ch. 4). The products generated by these efforts (technology and information) reflect particular configurations and distributions of state power and class power within national societies. Technological advances are determined within specific social settings.

The Politics of Agricultural Research

The influential induced innovation explanation of agricultural research activities, in its "pure" form, provides a pluralist political interpretation of agricultural research policymaking. Proponents of this model argue that private sector demand for and public sector supply of agricultural research are brought into equilibrium via a "political market" for public goods (Hayami and Ruttan 1985; Ruttan 1982; Binswanger and Ruttan 1978). Hayami and Ruttan (1971:57) summarize the induced innovation process as follows:

> Farmers are induced by shifts in relative prices to search for technical alternatives which save the increasingly scarce factors of production. They press the public research institutions to develop new technology and, also, demand that agricultural supply firms supply technical inputs which substitute for the more scarce factors. Receptive scientists and science administrators respond by making available new technical possibilities and new inputs that enable farmers to profitably substitute the increasingly abundant factors for increasingly scarce factors, thereby guiding the demand of farmers for unit cost reduction in a socially optimum direction.

Thus, the research process is receptive to a clientele that stands to gain economically from particular agricultural research programs.

The direct response of the state to societal interests depends on the degree of associational density in civil society and the ways in which demands of organized societal interests are channeled into the governmental decision-making process (e.g., conduits of effective influence within the executive, legislative, and/or administrative branches of the government). Hayami and Ruttan (1971) emphasize the deliberate "socialization" of agricultural research and extension (R & E) through responsive political structures. In their comparative study of technical change in agriculture in Japan and the United States, they stress that "resources for public sector R & E were obtained in a political marketplace and allocated through state-supported bureaucratic mechanisms," and that farmers "pressed" public research institutions to develop new technologies (Hayami and Ruttan 1971:35). Ruttan (1983:9) has recently stated that robust (and socially efficient) agricultural R & E systems depend "on the emergence of organized producer groups who are effective in bringing their interests to bear on legislative and executive budgetary processes."

Even in the pluralistic American polity, the above scenario skirts the pivotal role of state officials and nonfarm interests in organizing particular clientele groups during the formative stages of public sector agricultural R & E development in the United States. McConnell (1953), for example, notes that the leadership of the agricultural R & E movement was from the very outset divorced from the populist political program of the 1880s and 1890s. Rather, the leaders of the agricultural R & E movement were educators who took a dim view of the radical leanings of many small farmers. Many farmers were more interested in prices, credit, and nationalization of transportation, banking, and marketing sectors than in agricultural research.

Mobilization of political support for land-grant complex (the agricultural college and state experiment station systems) activities—in this case extension—is illustrated by the passage of the Smith-Lever Act in 1914. Seaman Knapp's institution building efforts show how the R & E system developed within a particular state/society milieu. With the aid of local Texas businessmen and some seed money from the General Education Board (supported in part by Rockefeller "philanthropic" funds), Knapp promoted the idea of the diffusion of new technology through a formal county extension agent network. This local innovation was nationalized with the passage of the Smith-Lever Act, which provided federal money for extension activities linked to land-grant agricultural education and research programs. According to McConnell (1953:30), a coalition of bankers, farm equipment manufacturers, and transportation companies lobbied strongly for "socialization" of extension work in the interest of a "contented" rural population. Gradual change through scientific farming and education was perceived as a productive alternative to agrarian populism that had frightened the power elite earlier.

Under the Smith-Lever legislation, the county agent worked under the aegis of a county farmer board. Agents organized farmer committees or "farm bureaus" (as they came to be known) to support extension programs. In effect, says McConnell (1953:47), "the county agent became the publicly paid organizer of the American Farm Bureau Federation." This organization, of course, became a strong farm interest group in twentieth century American politics. The Farm Bureau has lobbied effectively over the years for land-grant programs oriented toward the more prosperous, large farm segments of the American farming community. This process—the creation of a constituent organization by a government agency—smacks more of corporatism than pluralism. Lowi (1979:67-77) has described the end result of the process as "private expropriation of public authority." In this political setting, the pluralistic concept of government response to effective demand is somewhat misleading.

Danbom (1979) has gone even further in interpreting the American agricultural transformation in the direction of our argument—that agricultural research may become a mobilization tool employed by state agents to support the national industrialization effort. According to Danbom, cheap food and competitive efficiency were the paramount state bureaucratic goals for agriculture in the immediate post-World War I era. The evident correlation between industrialization and national power—which was reinforced by the war experience—led to conscious efforts on the part of the federal bureaucracy to push "Fordism" in American agriculture, thus overcoming wage goods' constraints and freeing more "inefficient" rural labor for factory work. Danbom (1979:140) argues:

> Not only did the war see an increase in production, it also enhanced the opportunity of the government to identify and organize those farmers most efficient and most likely to see the advantages of industrialization. Even after the war, when the American Farm Bureau Federation became a semiprivate pressure group, the government retained close ties with it because it was the farm organization most likely to agree with the urban critics that agricultural problems derived from rural inefficiency and demand industrial solutions. The Farm Bureau Federation gave those farmers most likely to embrace the modern ideals of organization and efficiency a say in the future of agricultural policy, but it also gave urban pressure groups and the federal government a means of dealing with agriculture.

The main point of this brief exposition of the American experience in establishing a public sector agricultural R & E complex is that, even in political systems where interest group politics is often thought to reign supreme in domestic affairs (if not in foreign policy), the resources of the state may be used to structure public sector organizations in directions favorable to bureaucrats themselves and/or powerful actors in society who will reap disproportionate gains from "socialization." Thus, agricultural research in the United States came to focus on productivity goals as sources of political support were consolidated. For the most part, economic and social structural issues have been avoided or viewed with outright hostility. Large-scale commercial farms became the primary clientele of the American agricultural research establishment.

If there is doubt about the grassroots political impetus for agricultural research programs in the United States, historical analysis of the Japanese agricultural development experience leads to even more questions about the relative weight of society- versus state-centered political initiatives, given the role of the state in Japan's latecomer industrialization effort (Johnson 1982). Hayami and Ruttan give an ambivalent account of the advance of agricultural technology and its institutionalization in research organizations in Japan in the late nineteenth and early twentieth centuries. Statements such as "the development of the agricultural experiment station in Japan was from its beginning characterized by strong initiatives from the national government" (Hayami and Yamada 1975:238) and improved production practices "were discovered by farmers and propagated by the itinerant instructors, and sometimes enforced by the sabres of the police" (Hayami and Ruttan 1971:157) clearly indicate that effective demand from farmers was not the only social factor instrumental in institutionalizing technical change in agriculture.

Hayami and Ruttan's (1971) discussion acknowledges the crucial role of agriculture in Meiji national development policy. There is widespread agreement that the Meiji restoration was a "revolution from above" by a fraction of the bureaucratic class whose power was based on political and military links to the Tokugawa feudal lords rather than on landed and/or commercial wealth (Skocpol 1979:100-104). This group was able to effect a centralized administrative governing structure under the aegis of the emperor. The goal of the Meiji bureaucrats was to build an industrial and military production base that would make Japan competitive in the international state system. In order to minimize foreign dependence during the development process, a strategy of internal mobilization of investment resources was emphasized.

The Meiji bureaucrats quickly swept aside the "feudal" social relations of production of the Tokugawa period.[2] A key change in the pattern of expropriation of the agricultural surplus was the conversion of a feudal land tax in kind to an annual money tax based on the assessed value of agricultural land. Until 1900, this tax constituted the principal revenue source of the central government and became the financial basis for government investment in a national industrial and military base (Ogura 1963:3). Many economic historians conclude that the abrogation of Tokugawa feudal relationships paved the way for a new era of Japanese agricultural development. Market incentives for increased production were finally unleashed from feudal fetters and new agricultural technologies and institutional innovations were adopted in response to economic opportunities.

As Ranis points out (1970:37-58), tax burdens caused many small peasant owner-operators who had received de facto title to land under the Meiji reforms to fall into tenancy due to their difficulty in meeting land tax obligations under conditions of widely fluctuating market prices for rice. Those who fell into tenancy paid rents in kind tied to current levels of production. Ranis (1970:45) says:

> There was no a priori necessity for the tenant to derive any benefits from the secular changes in prices and productivity. The burden of rents as a percentage of net output declined somewhat, especially in later years. Widening lags between increasing production and rents helped to strengthen incentives among tenant-tillers. However, the landlord clearly stood to gain the most from the exploitation of agricultural reserves of productivity. Receiving rising direct or rental incomes while paying taxes increasingly in smaller proportion, this group was in a position to lay claim to most of the surplus which did not land in government coffers.

This differential weight of incentives under an altered agrarian structure helps explain the key roles of the landlord-operators in diffusing new technologies (Sawada 1965:339-344). These key actors at the village level were able to put pressure on laggard peasants to adopt new technology recommendations by conscripting local authorities (the police) to force compliance. And since national development efforts financed by central government tax revenues were tied to the extraction of the agricultural surplus during the early Meiji period, the national government "socialized" private sector initiatives to promote new technology by promulgating such statutes as the Agricultural Association Law (1899). This law made membership in farmer improvement associations "compulsory for landowners and tenant cultivators" (Ogura 1963:7). It was apparently instituted to stimulate production in regions that had not taken advantage of new technical opportunities.

Thus, initiatives to develop state-supported agricultural research and extension programs appear to have come from both state officials and farmers. The farmer initiatives seem to have been confined largely to a narrow upper stratum, which gained disproportionately from the Meiji agricultural reforms. When the political party system waxed in the 1920s and the Diet (national legislature) became more responsive to popular demands from the agricultural sector, emphasis was placed on tenancy reform and securing independent title to the land. Mass political activity among farmers tended to coalesce around radical changes in agrarian structure rather than gradualist productivity-enhancing programs.

Closer scrutiny of the American and Japanese cases of agricultural development, exemplars in the induced innovation model of how politics and economics jointly effected socially efficient technical change in agriculture, has been necessary to bring the state back into the analysis as an independent force and to note the structure of effective demand from both the agricultural and nonagricultural sectors. As the induced innovation model was put to the test in other regions and historical periods, more realistic modifications were articulated to fit state/society relations which diverged markedly from pluralist ideals. An "impure" induced innovation variant arose to cope with the realization that skewed distributions of social power produce "distorted" economic and/or political markets in many societies. In fact, these two market imperfections are often causally interrelated—that is, powerful interests rig markets to obtain economic rents that would not accrue to them if assets and, hence, political power were more evenly distributed. Induced innovation responses in such social contexts are "impure" in the sense that misallocations of public sector agricultural R & E resources are likely to occur that do not reflect the real value of scarce resources in society and thus lead to suboptimal socioeconomic outcomes (Ruttan 1982; Sanders and Ruttan 1978).

While Hayami and Ruttan (1985:96) eschew a class-based interpretation of agricultural research activities, de Janvry and Dethier (1985:4-15) recast induced innovation in Neomarxian terms to reflect a logic of "class efficiency." The failure of agricultural research and extension to improve staple food production in much of Latin America is attributed to "disarticulated" social formations in which marginal, subsistence wage goods producers supply labor and "social insurance" to "peripheral" capitalists at very low costs (de Janvry 1981). Staple food production strategies for peasant producers are not registered in agricultural research programs because of class-based opposition to new technologies that might integrate marginal agricultural groups more fully into factor markets and thus threaten the extant social mode of control over the surplus. Thus, the state, as the collective rationalizing authority and/or the bureaucratic site of inter- and intraclass conflict within capitalist society (in this case a "disarticulated" peripheral capitalist society), responds to social power differentials in ways that support extant social relations. As a result, capital-intensive production systems may be promoted in labor surplus economies perpetuating agrarian dualism.

State officials may also act independently of (or even against) the interests of powerful classes and interest groups. de Janvry and Dethier (1985:12-13) recognize this possibility in their discussion of "The State Acting from Above." In most Neomarxist analysis, the state is only *conjuncturally* autonomous. That is, state autonomy appears only at particular moments of class paralysis (Marx's *18th Brumaire*) in capitalist social formations or during periods of class crystallization in peripheral areas being incorporated into a capitalist world system when a nascent bourgeoisie is still weak (Carnoy 1984, Ch. 7; Thomas 1984).

A state-centric argument, by contrast, emphasizes that potential state autonomy is an inherent structural feature of the modern world system. Relative capacities for state intervention vary across similar modes of production as the geopolitical, economic, and cultural dimensions of the modern world system change over time. From a developmental state perspective, agricultural research programs are calculated attempts by state agents to mobilize the private sector in support of a national project to achieve an effective competitive position within the world political economy (Johnson 1982, Ch. 1). The objectives of agricultural research policies are often closely tied to aggregate, macroeconomic goals such as food self-sufficiency and debt management that meliorate industrialization crises, rather than direct responses to demands of specific organized interest groups or class fractions.

It is argued here that induced innovation processual dynamics, in either their "pure" or "impure" (including class-based) formulations, do not adequately describe agricultural research policymaking in "inclusionary corporatist" or "exclusionary statist" state/society relationships.[3] In other words, there is a failure to incorporate adequately the possibilities of autonomous state action in discussions of agricultural research policy. If budgetary authority resides in state agencies rather than in the legislature, if the state bureaucracy is recruited from a narrow social stratum enabling it to maintain a sense of corporate separation from other societal groups, and/or if private interest groups have restricted access to bureaucratic organs, state officials have the capacity to act autonomously. In either inclusionary corporatist or exclusionary statist polities, state officials may possess the fiscal, coercive, and/or ideological means to act directly upon society—for instance, to regulate and/or mobilize interest articulation, to manipulate market structures, to lead public opinion. In the exclusionary political systems of certain NICs, agricultural research programs may best be described as "directed" innovation initiatives (Burmeister 1987a).

Induced or Directed Innovation? Implications for Development Theory

Contrasting alternative induced and directed innovation explanations of agricultural research and extension activities highlight an unresolved question in development theory, namely the nature of the interactive relation between the market and the state. The induced innovation position emphasizes the degree to which the state articulates the interests of individuals or groups. The state is basically an agent of society. State economic intervention occurs in agricultural research because the market as an institution does not supply adequate quantities of "collective" or "public" goods. The directed innovation perspective, in contrast, emphasizes the inherent ability of state officials to exercise control over the socioeconomic system through the deployment of administrative resources at their command. State officials may articulate and implement policies consonant with their definition of the public or national interest (Krasner 1978). These policy positions are not necessarily congruent with the interests of affected social groups.

In the induced innovation argument, agricultural research decisions are formed in a crucible of market-generated information about commodity values. The meaning of prices is crucial. Prices convey in a concise, codified signal essential information about what individuals want. The price mechanism is the most accurate gauge of revealed social preferences and, as such, provides an efficient way for individuals and groups to make decisions about the provision of public goods—in this case agricultural research.

Cross-national variations in state/society relationships are rendered increasingly superfluous as explanations of public sector economic activity due to the international expansion of markets. China represents the last serious attempt at autarkic development. The abandonment of that path signals the death knell for mercantilism as a national economic policy. Regardless of the domestic blend of market and administrative resource allocation mechanisms now found in the world's polities, state policymakers recognize with increasing regularity the need to adapt to international markets to procure resources and technologies that are in short supply. These resources are required as inputs to achieve a level of economic growth consistent with public expectations. Establishing the institutional parameters for satisfactory market performance has become perhaps the most important rationale for the state's existence in the twentieth century. If satisfactory performance is blocked by institutional rigidities, new arrangements will be effected by societal pressures for a reorganization of property, exchange, and/or authority relationships. These institutional adjustments that alter state policies in more facilitative directions flow from the growth possibilities rooted in economic "laws" of comparative advantage. People recognize that their increasing economic value is a function of the availability of alternative economic opportunities made possible by exchange relationships. In short, socioeconomic change is a response to positive-sum growth prospects. In the language of the induced innovation proponents, the prospects of increasing income streams induce political activity among those in a position to capture these gains. The positive-sum nature of economic growth means that all segments of society will eventually have the incentive to organize to improve their absolute levels of well-being.

Institutional innovations—for example, the provision of public goods such as agricultural research—are responses to these societal pressures.

The induced innovation proponents fail to reflect more seriously on the dark side of market operations and price determination—price fixing made possible by oligopolistic or monopolistic positions of control over markets. This possibility changes the meaning of price. In oligopolistic markets, prices are determined as much by relative power relationships linking a few key actors as by aggregate individual choice. Prices represent one party's ability to dictate favorable terms of trade.

The importance of this other concept of price has great bearing on the argument if one takes the position that market structures in the present "one world economy" gravitate much more toward the oligopolistic than the competitive pole (Feinberg 1983:109-127; Zysman 1983:32-46). If an international market for a product exists, new producer entrants must adapt to extant prices and standards. Existing producers have a variety of means to discourage new entrants. Because outcomes in an oligopolistic market are indeterminate—that is, are arrived at through bargaining—powerful allies may be required both to gain market entry and to meet competitive pressures. Given that trade is advantageous (or even necessary) for economic development, nations strive to become players on an international economic scene that is already populated by entrenched competitors. State resources are deployed in a variety of ways (direct state action or indirect private sector subsidization) in order to bring as much countervailing power as possible into the fray. Agricultural research activities become another policy tool in the state's arsenal of strategic economic interventions. This fact of twentieth century economic life has made state power more crucial in determining relative national economic well-being and has made the state/society relationship a key variable in the analysis of how nation-states fare in international economic competition—competition among units of varying economic strength under rules usually established by and for the benefit of the strongest (Wood 1986; Krasner 1985).

The emphasis placed in this chapter on variations in state/society relationships makes the market subordinate in certain historical situations to the preferences of state officials. State authorities have the power to create markets and influence the actions of those who participate in exchange activities. The internationalist vision (either in its liberal reformist or its revolutionary socialist guise) that worldwide economic exchange networks will effect the transformation of the interstate system into "one world" has yet to materialize. Chapter 3 chronicles the emergence of the exclusionary developmental state in postwar South Korea. The Korean directed innovation agricultural R & E response must be understood within the context of this particular state/society relationship. Attention is focused on how this relationship crystallized in reaction to both internal and external conflict on the geopolitically strategic Korean peninsula.

Notes

1. A recent discussion of the state/society relationship as a concept is provided by Migdal (1985). Collins (1968) outlines the domains of state and society as separate conceptual realms. Other discussions influential in the author's conceptualization of the state/society relationship include Giddens (1985); Buzan (1983, especially Ch. 2); Skocpol (1979:24-33); Stepan (1978, Chs. 1-2).

2. The nature of Japanese "feudalism" continues as a subject of lively scholarly debate among specialists. See Ogura (1963, Ch. 1) and Lockwood (1954:1-37, 549-556).

3. The literature on corporatism is useful in outlining the argument for potential state autonomy in state/society relationships. See, for example, Katzenstein (1978, 1985) and Chalmers (1985).

3
State and Society in Korea: Sociopolitical Context of Public Sector Investment in Agricultural Research

Collins (1986) has argued that buried within the Weberian corpus is a geopolitical theory of internal social structure that links what happens in the "power-prestige" arena of interstate competition to relations of social domination and processes of class formation at the national level. The notion that "politics works from the outside in" is emphasized in this chapter depicting the nature of the state/society relationship in Korea. It is argued that in the twentieth century exogenous social forces, first Japanese imperialism and then the Cold War, have created a statist mode of social domination in Korea. While interesting arguments have been made for important social structural and cultural continuities between state/society relations in precolonial Yi dynasty and postliberation Korea, these influences are of secondary importance compared to the weight of exogenous forces in the emergence of the post-World War II sociopolitical order. This position reflects the realities of Korean adaptation to difficult external circumstances. Fate in the guise of geographical location has not been kind to the Korean people.

This chapter begins with a brief overview of the external pressures that have shaped the Korean social structure. The discussion then moves chronologically to explore briefly how exogenous political control—first, subjugation under the Japanese Empire and then the brief postwar American military occupation interlude—established important patterns in social power relationships that have carried over into the postindependence period. The crystallization of the state/society relationship in the Republic of Korea is described, with special attention focused on the social landscape of the countryside that will be the primary concern in our discussion of the technical change process in agriculture. Finally, this chapter concludes with a discussion of whether the present state/society relationship can be traced back to the precolonial social structure of the Yi dynasty; that is, whether social dynamics internal to Korean society have been underemphasized in our account of the emergence of the current "pact of social domination."[1]

The International Nexus of Contemporary Korean Politics

The postcolonial breakup of Korea has few historical parallels. Vietnam is now reunited. The two Germanys have forged diplomatic links as a result of Willy Brandt's Ostpolitik. In Korea, however, a unified nation has been split into two antagonistic states that to this day proscribe even postal contact. That the centuries-old peninsular political unity was severed in such absolute terms is a testament to the tenacious internalization of Cold War divisions in a geopolitically strategic third world region.

The development of postliberation state/society relations in South Korea cannot be discussed outside of the context of the North-South division. As Kihl (1984) argues, internal division has fueled state aggrandizement in both Koreas. Internal politics continue to be fashioned in a reactive maelstrom of North-South competition for peninsular hegemony and international recognition. State power finds its material and organizational manifestations most dramatically reflected in the top-heavy military sector that maintains a predominant position within the state apparatus in both Koreas (Kim 1984). The contrast between postcolonial militarist, activist states on both sides of the demilitarized zone (DMZ) and the rather pacific, isolationist, nondevelopmental state of the precolonial Yi dynasty is stark indeed (Palais 1975). Korea is a classic case of how the internal social structure of third world societies has been influenced by world system dynamics.

The support of the superpowers appears to have been crucial in the establishment of governing authorities in both the North and the South. The relative weight of indigenous social forces and external assistance in forging political consolidation in the North under the aegis of the North Korean Workers' Party (NKWP) led by Kim Il Sung is still an open question.

The ruthless suppression of the indigenous Korean independence movement by the Japanese colonial authorities drove many opposition groups into exile. *Within* Korea, it now appears that the communist movement had the strongest organizational base of any opposition group at the time of liberation (Matray 1985), due primarily to its organizational structure of clandestine cells. This organizational structure was better adapted to evade infiltration by colonial government authorities and their legions of informants. However, local communist leaders were often forced out or "eliminated" in intraparty power struggles immediately following the withdrawal of the Japanese from Korea. Kim Il Sung apparently spent the 1940s in the Soviet Union and Manchuria as an intelligence officer in the Soviet army (Kihl 1984). This background suggests key linkages between Kim and Soviet military occupation officials during the initial postindependence period of political consolidation, implying a heavy external imprint on NKWP activities and successes. Significant military and economic assistance from the Soviet bloc flowed into North Korea after the official establishment of the Korean Democratic People's Republic in the North (Kihl 1984:154-155). At present, the cult of "Kim Il Sungism" prevents serious investigations of the nationalist roots of Kim's brand of Korean communism.

American interference in the South is more transparent and will be analyzed in some detail later on. In any event, superpower intervention effectively blocked ongoing internal struggles among competing political factions to unify the Korean peninsula under a single governing authority. Subsequent analysis in this monograph focuses on what happened in the South. In the South, in particular, a colonial imprint was stamped on postindependence political accommodations.

The State and the Countryside in Colonial Korea

The thoroughness of bureaucratic control and economic integration separates the Japanese colonial experience from its European analogues. As Cumings (1984b) explains, lateness in "world time," the dense populations of the territories colonized, and historical legacies of contact (and conflict) account for much of the difference. As was mentioned earlier, Japanese industrialization was, in large part, a response to external threats to national sovereignty. Cumings (1984b:482) emphasizes that

Japanese state officials, in the wake of a humiliating capitulation to European concession-seekers in the midnineteenth century, perceived their country as "disadvantaged and threatened by the more advanced countries." Serious efforts to achieve parity with the established colonial powers led to the annexation of contiguous East Asian territories as soon as Japan became industrially and militarily capable of waging interstate warfare. Following the Japanese military victories over the major Asian continental powers, China and Russia, at the turn of the century, Japan constructed a colonial territorial defense perimeter consisting of Taiwan, Korea, and later Manchuria and proceeded to integrate these annexed territories into the Japanese economy in a systematic fashion. Dense populations and antagonistic historical legacies led to the initial administration of the colonies by Japanese military officials. Japanese rule called forth a sustained program to develop colonial industry and agriculture in support of the metropole's industrial development and military objectives. The geographical proximity of the colonies facilitated the flow of both goods and people. Japanese expatriates (entrepreneurs, engineers, farmers) established modern agricultural and industrial enterprises in the colonies. And the community control apparatus set up by the military administration was utilized in direct support of these economic mobilization efforts (Chen 1984:227-235). Tight economic integration coupled with centralized administrative control accounts for the Janus-faced nature of the Japanese colonial experience. Valuable infrastructure was created which provided a solid foundation for postwar economic growth in Korea and Taiwan, but the accompanying legacy of political (and attempted cultural) control was bitterly resented, especially in Korea. The Japanese were blamed for all of Korea's subsequent postwar development problems (division of the peninsula, unequal economic exchange relations, political underdevelopment, etc.), while at the same time the postwar ruling elite left the Japanese administrative structure intact to consolidate their own fragile control over recalcitrant social forces.

The dialectic of colonial economic development and political control is illustrated by colonial agricultural sector programs. Sagging agricultural productivity in Japan eventually led to a wage goods bottleneck and rising rice prices. An ensuing political crisis culminated in the rice riots of 1918, a turning point in Japanese political awareness of the social volatility of the country's rapid industrialization program. Increasingly, Taiwan and Korea were tapped as alternative rice suppliers in an effort to keep a lid on the price of essential wage goods, thus supporting the industrialization process by minimizing cost of living increases for the growing working class.

A colonial solution to a serious bottleneck in the capital accumulation process was facilitated by ecological similarities between the colonies and the metropole. Appropriate, improved technology for rice production, developed earlier in Japan, could be introduced directly in Korea. Hayami and Ruttan (1985: 280-292) chronicle the process of technology transfer and infrastructural improvement (especially irrigation facilities). A dense agrobureaucracy with effective penetration power spread the new technology widely throughout the Korean peninsula. Extension agents activated a colonial government-landlord alliance similar to the previously noted early Meiji accommodation that assured the adoption of improved rice varieties, the application of fertilizer, and the improvement of irrigation systems. Control over land resources passed inexorably into the hands of landlords, both Korean and expatriate Japanese. Grajdanzev (1944:112) reported that in 1932, landlord families constituting 3.7% of all farm families controlled 63.9% of the cultivable land in Korea, including most of the prime agricultural land. This group had a strong political and economic predisposition to follow the instructions of colonial government research and extension personnel relating to infrastructural development and the adoption of improved technology. Obstreperous tenants were brought into line by local gendarmes, if necessary.

The majority of farm families were losing ground even as aggregate agricultural production was increasing. The gradual loss of control over land resources was mirrored by declines in per capita food consumption in the countryside. During the period from 1915 to 1933, per capita rice consumption in Korea decreased by approximately 35% and per capita consumption of all cereals, the mainstay of the Korean diet, decreased by approximately 20% (Grajdanzev 1944:119). Landlessness and the increased severity of the traditional "spring famine" (the period preceding the harvest of the winter cereals when rice stocks had run out) were the direct results of an extractive foodgrains policy promulgated to support the Japanese industrial and military buildup.

Peasant unrest swelled throughout the 1930s in response to the colonial politics of productivity and distribution. So-called "red peasant unions" carried out hit-and-run guerrilla operations against Japanese authorities and Korean collaborators. Rural unrest generated by extant land tenancy and grain confiscation arrangements festered throughout the waning days of the empire and carried over into the independence period. State intervention in agricultural production and marketing still evokes complaints from Korean farmers, based on the bitter legacy of colonial surplus extraction policies.

The American Military Government in Korea

Disposition of colonial possessions was an important agenda item in the big power summits of World War II. Unfortunately for Koreans, events on the ground outran negotiations. Previously discussed trusteeship arrangements had not been codified prior to the Japanese surrender in August, 1945. With Soviet troops massed at the Korean-Manchurian border, a quick decision was made in the U.S. State Department to divide the peninsula into American and Soviet administrative zones at the thirty-eighth parallel. Plans for a joint U.S.-U.S.S.R. trusteeship and reunification program were to be worked out in subsequent negotiation sessions. The superimposition of Cold War occupation and negotiation conflicts upon fractious, indigenous Korean political struggles eventually culminated in the Korean War, a conflation of civil war with international geopolitical conflict that defies easy historical interpretation (Cumings 1981, 1983; Matray 1985). The result was a permanently divided Korea.

In the South, an American military government (AMG) was assembled quickly from other military units stationed in the Far East, principally Okinawa. Liberation from the Japanese occurred in August, 1945. U.S. forces did not arrive on the peninsula until September. In the interim, the prominent leftist leader Yoe Un-Hyeong struck a deal with outgoing Japanese colonial officials for the formation of a transitional government. In return for protecting Japanese lives during the evacuation of Japanese expatriates from Korea, Japanese colonial officials recognized Yoe's group as the interim governing authority. Matray elaborates (1985:48):

Yoe promptly set about creating local "people's

committees" (an unfortunate designation) to assume administrative responsibilities. Most leaders accepted Yoe's authority, including landlords, intellectuals, students, and professional people. Moreover, Yoe's 135 committees were able to exploit the Japanese communication, transportation, and administration network, rapidly achieving a measurable amount of centralized power. The people's committees quickly expropriated the land of the Japanese and their Korean collaborators, while simultaneously releasing all political prisoners. By the end of August, Yoe had emerged as the unchallenged de facto leader throughout Korea.

The local people's committees represented a broad range of nationalist, socialist, and communist positions on the political spectrum. Communist party representation was strong. As was mentioned earlier, communist underground activity had been the most organized anticolonial resistance force within Korea. Henderson (1968:320-322) claims that, at liberation, the communist party was "unquestionably the country's most single important political force." In any event, a true social revolution was underway in the countryside. The extant colonial edifice was collapsing rapidly. Indigenous Korean collaborators were being singled out for retribution. Social confusion was exacerbated by a rapid influx of Koreans returning to their home areas following military service or forced labor in other parts of the Empire. For many, this experience was a personal passage from peasantry to proletariat, undoubtably a radicalizing life experience (Cumings 1981).

On September 6, 1945, Yoe proclaimed the establishment of the Korean People's Republic (KPR), a national governing umbrella for the local people's committees. Committees were moving quickly to confiscate and redistribute colonial and collaborator assets. Land was redistributed to peasant cultivators and factories were handed over to workers' councils organized under the auspices of the people's committees. These revolutionary actions had taken place in the interval *before* the AMG arrived in the South. Such actions, of course, generated widespread popular support for the KPR, its program, and the local committee affiliates.

The intervention of the AMG in the South provided conservative Korean landlords and middle-level Korean bureaucrats who had served the colonial regime with a source of countervailing power in a rapidly deteriorating political situation. For reasons both practical and ideological, AMG authorities did not recognize the KPR as a legitimate indigenous Korean political channel for negotiation or control. AMG officials tried to abrogate the authority of the people's committees in local areas, by force if necessary. In order to impose control, local authorities who had served during the Japanese occupation were reinstated and armed. Particularly galling to most Koreans was the reinstatement of the hated national police. For all practical purposes, this policy amounted to retention of the Japanese colonial administrative structure and many of its Korean staff. For many collaborators, it was a godsend. The tainted native Korean power elite received vital external support at a crucial period of incipient social revolution. Some changes, such as the momentum toward land reform, could not be undone. But the stage was set for the reimposition of centralized, authoritarian political rule necessary to maintain order and to rollback the revolutionary thrust of the KPR agenda.

The bureaucratic structure imposed through AMG intervention looked suspiciously similar to colonial bureaucratic arrangements, both in terms of modus operandi and personnel. Both within the U.S. and within conservative political circles in Korea, the specter of communist domination of the peninsula loomed more likely, as political accommodations reminiscent of Eastern European experiences began to take shape in the minds of those most threatened by revolutionary change. The influx of conservative leaders and Christian refugees from the North, whose lives and property were threatened by the political consolidation of an increasingly unified NKWP apparatus, provided further momentum in the South for a conservative counterthrust.

The AMG was continually frustrated by Korean internal politics. Rather than promote a unified front coalition which would have, of necessity, contained a significant leftist and communist component, AMG authorities searched for a moderate-conservative nationalist coalition. Ironically, circumstances forced the U.S. to back the aged independence crusader Syngman Rhee. In the course of bilateral negotiations with the Soviets over occupation and unification issues, Rhee, in effect, repeatedly sabotaged U.S. plans to promote compromise among Korean political leaders over reunification issues by refusing to participate in discussions with contending rivals in the North and the South, claiming that any delay in granting Korean independence (e.g., a U.N. Trusteeship) and unification was an unconscionable extension of colonial rule in Korea. Rhee's refusal to participate made it difficult for U.S. negotiators to mobilize a conservative counterweight to the inevitable leftist political challenge in any unification format. But by taking an unyielding, dogmatic position on the unification issue, Rhee did stake out a nationalist position with widespread popular appeal. As plans for eventual U.S. withdrawal from the South developed, Rhee was the only conservative leader of national stature who had mobilized enough political support to lead a conservative government.

Postindependence Political Consolidation

The Republic of Korea (ROK) under President Syngman Rhee was officially proclaimed on August 15, 1948. Initially, Rhee's position was quite precarious. Even within moderate and conservative circles his political base was insecure. Open revolt faced the government in many rural areas (Merrill 1983). Thus, from the start, Rhee was forced to rely on internal security forces, often led and staffed by people with collaborationist pasts, to eliminate dissidents and restore civil order. Rhee's political supporters were a shifting coalition of favor-seekers. During his tenure (1948-1960), he failed to institutionalize civilian politics. Important social groups—classes, interest groups, political parties—were not incorporated into government decision-making processes in any permanent, structured fashion.

Although the basic political tenor of the regime was consevative, Rhee could not avoid promulgating a thoroughgoing land reform starting in 1949. As stated earlier, declines in rural living conditions and associated rural unrest led to a socially volatile situation in the countryside prior to liberation (Grajdanzev 1944). Land reform was the predominant item on the agenda of the people's committees (Cumings 1981:33-34, 78). The AMG's reinstatement of local government officials who served under colonial rule stopped indigenous redistribution. But the example of North Korea's land reform in 1946, coupled with procrastination by governing authorities in the South, fueled continuing rural unrest.

Rhee's reluctance to push for further redistribution courted open civil strife. However, he was finally persuaded that land reform was crucial to his political survival. The reform had significant levelling effects on the rural power structure. Owner-operators were limited to three-hectare holdings, and tenancy was proscribed. A landlord-tenant system controlled by a landed aristocracy gave way to a unimodal agrarian structure of small landholders (Johnston and Kilby 1975). Old entrenched agricultural interests no longer possessed well-established channels to the center of power. And the leaders of the ascendant leftist forces either were killed, fled to the North, or were driven underground as rightist forces gradually gained control of the countryside following sporadic, abortive uprisings against government officials that began under the AMG in the autumn of 1946. Periodic purges of leftists occurred from that point in time until the end of the Korean War. The countryside was, in a sense, politically sanitized.

The social and political consequences of land reform mirrored a general trend toward a more fluid class structure. Even though the Japanese colonial period had been characterized by rapid industrial development and significant improvements in agricultural production capacity, Koreans were, for the most part, blocked from participation in these new sources of wealth accumulation. Neither a strong landed elite nor a powerful entrepreneurial class was present to make claims upon the state at the founding of the ROK. The physical destruction of assets accompanying the Korean War reinforced this social fluidity.

Perhaps a new aristocracy did emerge in the latter part of the Rhee era. Individuals who gained privileged access to aid dispersement channels, import-export licenses, and military service contracts for U.S. forces—high ranking bureaucrats, military officers, and Rhee's Liberal Party cronies—had the best opportunities to amass wealth through speculation and corruption. But this group was an ephemeral elite and was easily manipulated without causing social and economic upheaval.

The degree of continuity in the class structure from the colonial period to the formation of a nascent bourgeoisie in the Rhee years is now the subject of considerable scholarly interest. Most historical accounts emphasize the weakness of the entrepreneurial impetus during the 1950s. Speculation through access to monopoly rights over foreign exchange and import privileges are often cited as the preferred means of wealth accumulation during that era. However, new historical evidence challenging this position is beginning to surface (Jones and Sakong 1980; Moskowitz 1982). In any case, elite entrenchment in Korean society appears to have been relatively weak due to the confiscation of the property of preliberation "collaborators," further destruction of assets in the Korean War, and the failure of the Rhee government to support productive entrepreneurial ventures. Class structures based on accumulation of property and organizational power had not crystallized during the Rhee period.

The Rhee regime collapsed in the spring of 1960. Blatant election fraud was the immediate catalyst; but Rhee's senility, his inability to create an effective political organization to oversee a transfer of power to a new generation of leaders, and economic stagnation were major underlying factors (Henderson 1968:168-182; Kim 1971, Ch. 2). The more open parliamentary system of the Chang Myon interregnum (April, 1960-May, 1961) that followed was plagued from the start by fierce infighting among shifting coalitions of legislative factions. The government's ability to foster workable agreements on key political and economic issues facing the nation waned over time. More threatening in the short term was the incipient breakdown of those organizations responsible for maintaining civil order. The national police force had suffered public humiliation during the last Rhee days. And the military had refused to obey executive orders to fire on student demonstrators in Rhee's last efforts to quell the uprising against the regime. Ongoing legislative inquiries into the abuses of personal power by the highest ranking military officers enhanced the upward mobility prospects for the disgruntled reform-minded junior officers untainted by scandal, but at the same time threatened to undermine the unity and morale of the military.

During the Rhee era of political nondevelopment, the South Korean military had emerged as the most powerful national institution. The military had grown exponentially during the Korean War to troop levels of 600,000 that were maintained for national security reasons thereafter. However, the growing political cloud shrouding the military threatened to erode its influence in government circles thus reducing its power prerogatives and perquisites. These trends caused alarm among an emerging leadership cadre of middle-level military officers linked by ties of shared combat experiences, common political grievances against the "Rhee generals," and frustrations over lack of promotion opportunities (Kim 1971, Ch. 3; Kwon

1974).

Rumors of North Korean infiltration and sabotage efforts increased during the Chang Myon period. Students, intellectuals, and other left-leaning activists were permitted to enter the political fray and quickly began to clamor for prompt reunification negotiations, a neutral foreign policy, and an autarkic economic development strategy. Student leaders and their allies announced they were prepared to meet with North Korean counterparts to prepare the way for unconditional reunification talks. Negotiations initiated by such groups on terms over which the military had little control were a frightening prospect to activist military officers determined to play a role in deciding the nation's future. A military coup followed.

The military coup coincided with a rapidly deteriorating economic situation. Inflation continued to soar, economic output declined, and unemployment increased. Jobless university graduates became interested in "radical" political and economic fixes. The military coup leaders proclaimed reinvigorated commitment to economic mobilization and growth. They denigrated the abject dependency relationships with the United States that were felt by many to have marked the Rhee era. Exhortations advocating more vigorous and self-contained economic policy measures captured some of the sentiment of economic nationalism evoked in the protests of students and intellectuals.

As a social group, the military coup leaders did not have strong ties to the traditional rural aristocracy or the urban elites based in Seoul. A number (including Park Chung-Hee) came from modest rural backgrounds. Cole and Lyman (1971:35) comment:

> The military in Korea, if less alienated, was nevertheless still not accepted in Korean culture as an honored group nor as an accepted source for the ruling class. Traditionally, as in most Confucian-influenced societies, the military occupied a relatively low role in the social hierarchy. The military establishment had never been either large or influential throughout most of Korean history and had been allowed to decline to extremely low levels of men and materials by the beginning of the twentieth century. After independence and even after the

Korean War, when the general prestige of the military had risen, it continued to be a career opportunity for lesser privileged members of society. Officers rose primarily from families with money to provide their children with some education and assistance, but which lacked the entree to the best schools and universities of Seoul, where elite careers were normally fashioned.

Social isolation of this ruling group from other elite groups (particularly landlords-turned-entrepreneurs and the intelligentsia) is a key structural feature of the postcoup polity. Moreover, the concentration by General-turned-President Park of governmental power within the executive branch and its administrative agencies further removed state from society. This conscious consolidation of prerogatives within the executive branch enabled Park to circumvent possible opposition from the legislature based on interest articulation and independent party initiatives. This early establishment of executive hegemony, combined with the ability to rely on loyal agencies of coercion (e.g., the threat of imposing martial law and/or employing physical violence if political opponents threatened state authority), gave the Park regime the power to push through key economic and political changes against the will of vested interests and public opinion in general. Examples include reneging on promises to implement an "agriculture first" policy, threatening economic elites with confiscation of wealth and prison sentences if they refused to follow the prescribed disposition of their assets (e.g., the promulgation of the Illicit Wealth Accumulation Law), and the move to establish diplomatic and commercial relations with Japan.

Policymaking in this bureaucratic-authoritarian regime was the prerogative of the highest administrative echelons. The president took a great personal interest in many economic development initiatives. As Cole and Lyman (1971) and Lee (1968) emphasize, the military regime replaced Rhee's emphasis on nationalism and reunification with economic development as the *raison d'etre* for rule. Although national security and reunification were continually emphasized and used to justify draconian measures to clamp down on political dissent, the Rhee hope of quick reunification gave way to a more pragmatic goal of economic competition with the North as a means to reunification in the distant future. Victory in a "development war" superceded political reunification by force as the means to peninsular domination in the minds of Park and his close advisors.

To accomplish economic goals, the bureaucracy was purged (Lee 1968). Maximization of aid as the bureaucratic goal was replaced by effective allocation of resources to achieve economic targets. Policymaking was viewed as a technocratic, rather than political, exercise. Many of the high-ranking military officers who served initially in key government posts had obtained specialized training in modern management procedures as a result of their contact with United States military operations (many received special training abroad). And civilian expertise was sought for specialized government positions, especially in economic planning and finance. As befits a military regime, a command center (the president and his closest aides headquartered at the Blue House) issued plans and set targets. Plan implementation was carefully monitored by the president and the subordinate bureaucracy. Noncompliance or poor performance could then be identified expeditiously and appropriate countermeasures taken.

Economic affairs were consciously upgraded to first rank in President Park's hierarchy of policy concerns. Organizationally, this change became manifest in the consolidation of economic planning and coordination functions under the aegis of a new "superministrial" body, the Economic Planning Board (EPB). The chair of this agency was given Deputy Prime Minister standing in the cabinet with direct access to the Blue House. In effect, the EPB was an insulated bureaucratic organization through which the plans, programs, and budgets of the functional government ministries were approved, coordinated, and monitored.

The regime suppressed popular and special interest initiatives in policymaking. The legislature had little countervailing power. Legislation was initiated from the executive rather than from the legislative branch, and the legislature had no meaningful budgetary authority. Local government operations were directed from the central Ministry of Home Affairs. Even the weak local initiatives permitted under the Rhee regime were proscribed. Local or functional interests, then, had no formal institutionalized channels to government (Cho 1972; Aqua 1974).

It is in this political context that the agricultural research and extension organization in South Korea, the Office of Rural

Development (ORD)—recently renamed the Rural Development Administration—was established in 1962. In fact, this organization predates the "civilianization" of Park's rule in 1963. Initiatives for its establishment were taken by a development-oriented elite, not induced from below by local and/or popular pressures on government officials for new approaches to increasing productive capacity. Past experience with the agrobureaucracy, both during the Japanese colonial period and after liberation, was more exploitative than facilitative for the majority of farmers. Policies had been designed to increase the flow of agricultural products to government distributive channels at onerous terms of exchange. Farmers were undoubtably chary about any new central government initiatives.

The Social Landscape of the Countryside

Moskowitz (1982) and Apthorpe (1979) have emphasized a much neglected point in their discussions of the socioeconomic implications of land reforms in Korea and Taiwan. While these were cases of "integral" land reforms in the sense that the landed aristocracy was excised as a rural power elite (de Janvry 1984), the reforms were state controlled. A power void was created by land reform measures, and state authorities took advantage of this opportunity to create bonds of dependency between a relatively homogeneous group of minifarm owner-operators and a new surrogate landlord—the state agrobureaucracy. Land reform connoted neither the range of economic choice nor the political voice that is often attributed to it in the development literature.

While it may be true that land reform unleashes a burst of productivity in the countryside (this axiom is still hotly disputed among agricultural economists), the benefits of land reform are problematic without the provision of adequate production inputs and marketing services to those who gain title to the land. Landlords often provided credit and other essential inputs in the prereform days. In the post-land reform era, the state, at least initially, must step in to take up the slack. In many cases, the state as surrogate landlord is placed in a quite favorable position to extract a surplus from agricultural producers. In agrarian societies, this may be the only way to generate internally the resources needed to support state programs—both current expenditures and development initiatives. This post-land reform scenario occurred in both Korea and

Taiwan, as policy instruments such as terms of trade for agricultural products and industrial goods (including agricultural production inputs) and outright grain requisition edicts were used to effect an intersectoral transfer of resources.

In Korea, in particular, state agents moved to prevent political organization and interest articulation in the countryside. Blatant political motives were partly responsible; rural areas had been hotbeds of antigovernment activities from the 1930s on. The specter of peasant social revolution looms large in the twentieth century. While the threat of overt rural unrest was gradually quelled during the late 1940s and early 1950s, political sanitation measures were institutionalized with the takeover of local government functions by the Ministry of Home Affairs and its focus on organizational mobilization of peasant political and economic life (Kihl 1979). State economic leverage ensured a good deal of political control in the countryside.

Wade (1982, 1983) and Moore (1984, 1985) have done much to set the record straight in this regard. Wade has noted the extent to which the structure of state bureaucratic penetration prevents the articulation of grassroots political concerns and economic interests. Two illustrations suffice. The most important agrobureaucratic agency in the countryside is the octopus-like National Agricultural Cooperatives Federation (NACF) (see Steinberg, et al. 1984). This centrally-directed parastatal agency provides subsidized rural credit, monopolizes fertilizer sales and distribution, and markets important commodities to name three of its most important functions. After the Park takeover, the NACF was reorganized with branch offices dealing directly with farmers consolidated at the township (*myon*) jurisdiction level. The *myon* is an artificial administrative unit imposed by the central government on the social fabric of the countryside. Previous to this reorganization, NACF activities had been organized at the village level where social solidarity mechanisms often existed. When the central government decided to use the village as a program unit, as was the case with the highly publicized rural development effort in the 1970s (the New Community Movement [NCM] or *Saemaul Undong* in Korean), villages were positioned against one another as competitors for scarce NCM resources. The reward system of the NCM campaign was deliberately fashioned to downplay intervillage cooperation, even though it seems likely that many infrastructural improvement and income-generating projects would have benefitted from intervillage cooperation and economies of scale. Wade and Moore both argue that the NACF and NCM programs reflect the deliberate political and economic atomization of the countryside by the state.

In Wade's apt phrase, dependency relations were established so that central authorities could manage the Korean agricultural sector as "one farm." Independent minifarm operators with limited economic collateral and minimal political influence came to rely almost exclusively on the state agrobureaucracy for the provision of essential services. Through state agencies such as the NACF, agriculture could be steered in directions consonant with national macroeconomic goals and needs. Structural dependence creates its own dynamic of political clientelism. Rural areas became the bastions of government party support due to the efficacy with which scarce resources could be channeled into the countryside at election time. Government largesse in times of political crises (e.g., the need for electoral legitimation) assumes added importance when there are few other organized channels of interest articulation available.

As will be argued in the next chapter, there were sufficient economic benefits associated with government agricultural policy in the context of agrarian structural change (land reform) to bring the agricultural sector into national economic life in an "articulated" way. That is, both labor and wage goods were transferred to industry without pauperizing and marginalizing substantial portions of the agrarian population. This is a significant achievement as Hyden (1983) and de Janvry (1981) have recently reminded us. The key in Korea lies in a state/society relationship in which a strong state faces a weakly organized society. Land reform excised a potentially obstructionist landed aristocracy, the root of the Latin American "disarticulated" response to industrialization (de Janvry 1981). Political exclusion prevented a fragmented, small landholder agrarian sector from mounting serious political challenges to state-directed agricultural policy interventions designed to transfer labor and wage goods to the industrial sector. On the industrial side, the nascent bourgeoisie remained dependent on state credit and other inducements for expansion in a hothouse environment where the state played a leading entrepreneurial role in charting a national industrialization course (Barone 1983:61). This social landscape, as subsequent agricultural research policy analysis reveals, provided a propitious background for carrot-and-stick policies that were effective in mobilizing agriculture in support of industrialization. Before moving to this analysis, a brief discussion of "internalist" explanations of the statist mode of social domination in Korea is presented.

Historical Continuities in Statist Domination?

The preceding argument is basically an "externalist" explanation of the roots of the current exclusionist, statist mode of social domination in Korea. Emphasis was placed on the impact of world system dynamics on the internal political structure—particularly the "militarization" of the state apparatus and the economic development response to interstate competition between "regimes in contest" (Kihl 1984) in the North and the South. Other scholars have taken a more "internalist" tack in their interpretations of the Korean state/society relationship. Korea, unlike many third world nations, had a long continuous history of nationhood preceding Japanese colonization. Thus, many scholars argue that important vestiges of social structure and political culture left by the long-lived Yi dynasty (1392-1910) must be factored into any discussion of politics and society in Korea.

The most obvious point of departure is an "oriental despotism" parallel between precolonial Korea and the current authoritarian state apparatus. Marx and Wittfogel, among others, pioneered a bureaucratic centralist interpretation of the heavily populated, irrigation-dependent agrarian Asian societies and contrasted this social formation with the contemporaneous feudal social formation in Western Europe, where local, competing centers of power in the countryside (a landed nobility) and the towns were crystallizing in a way that would generate a regional political economy based on the interactive dynamics of interstate and capitalist competition. Although Korea became a "tributary vassal state" of the Chinese Empire in the premodern era, the state/society relationship in Yi dynasty Korea did not resemble that of a centralized, bureaucratic state that penetrated deeply into agrarian society.

While the Korean monarchy was theoretically an absolutist one, royal power was constrained in important ways by an aristocratic class (the *Yangban*) whose privileges were anchored in a combination of inherited landholding positions in the countryside and state officeholding (Palais 1975). These dual social loci of *Yangban* position had the effect of minimizing royal penetration into the countryside, while at the same time encouraging *Yangban*s to take up periodic residence at the royal court in Seoul to keep their state officeholding credentials current. This relationship with the center (state officeholding enmeshed in the civil service examination system) limited the ability and the interest of *Yangban* in the establishment of local centers of power from which to challenge royal authority. Furthermore, the balance of power between the monarchy and the aristocracy was grounded ideologically in Confucian precepts of the social order with its cosmology of idealized superordinate-subordinate social relationships which checked, through numerous structural mechanisms such as censorate monitoring of royal actions, efforts to effect social domination by either group.

Henderson (1968) adds an interesting twist to this reading of Yi dynasty social relationships in his seminal interpretation of late nineteenth century social dynamics. He argues that *Yangban* credentials had become blurred to the point where many more people were making claims to *Yangban* status that were difficult to refute. As a result, this fluid social environment produced a social scramble for a limited number of state offices, leading to endless struggles for position among those claiming elite *Yangban* status. Personal infighting for position was encouraged at the expense of progammatic initiatives. The political preoccupation with factional struggles sapped the energies of the Korean elite leading to debilitating social stasis on the peninsula.

This unproductive "balance of power" standoff intensified during the period of mounting external threats to Korean national autonomy. The Confucian cosmology posited the social superiority of those peoples incorporated under the Chinese "Mandate of Heaven." However, xenophobic isolationism was not a viable political response to foreign gunboat diplomacy. An attempt by the regent Yi Ha-Eung (the *Taewongun* or Grand Prince) in the 1870s to mobilize a central government response to impending external threats was stymied by internal social opposition to an enhancement of powers of the royal court. Neither an adequate military buildup nor an economic development push could be mounted. Korea's special relationship to the Chinese Empire offered no protection as the decaying Manchu dynasty was similarly impotent in the face of military and economic incursions by the European powers and Japan. China's defeat in the Sino-Japanese War (1898) left

Korea defenseless, generating a pathetic response in the first decade of the twentieth century wherein the Korean royal court tried to curry favor with the Russian and Japanese legations in Seoul in order to find a substitute for Chinese "protection." Needless to say this strategy was woefully inadequate in the face of the territorial expansion of the great powers prior to World War I. The contrast between a militarily prostrate Korea at the turn of the century and the present situation of the two Koreas, armed to the teeth, facing off at the DMZ is stark indeed, and raises serious questions about historical social structural continuities in the statist mode of social domination in Korea.

Notes

1. This phrase is employed by Cardoso and Faletto (1979) in their discussion of social power relationships in third world societies.

4
Korea's Green Revolution: Rice Research as State Development Policy

The rice self-sufficiency policy initiative during the 1970s was promulgated by the state to support the national industrialization project. In this chapter, the Office of Rural Development's (ORD) "green revolution" program is analyzed in depth. Technical decisions about the production and diffusion of new rice varieties are explained as responses to the social, economic, and political realities of Korea's state-directed industrialization push. Agricultural research decisions took place within the social matrix outlined in the previous chapter; policy responses were reactions to specific macroeconomic and political problems confronting state managers.

The Development and Diffusion of an Improved Rice Variety[1]

The Japanese introduced many improved rice varieties into Korea during the colonial period (1910-1945). Simultaneously, they started breeding varieties in Korea with the establishment of an agricultural demonstration farm in 1906, even before the official colonial annexation of the territory. Gradually, these introduced (Japanese) and improved (developed in Korea) varieties replaced the many indigenous varieties that were grown in earlier years. Before the inauguration of the green revolution campaign, the Office of Rural Development recommended twelve Korean improved varieties and nine introduced varieties from Japan for regional cultivation in Korea (Kim 1979:11). Although South Korea is a small country, important regional differences do exist for rice production. The north and central areas are susceptible to cold temperature damage. Specific pest problems have traditionally been associated with the Honam (southwest) and Yeongnam (southeast) regions. These differences, along with soil variation, fluctuations in water supplies due to variations in irrigation system quality, and double cropping variations, which require different planting and harvesting cycles, led to a sizeable number of location-specific varietal recommendations.

The varieties cultivated were all of the japonica type—short-statured, photoperiod sensitive, cold tolerant types adapted to temperate zone rice production.[2] With the release of the blast resistant Jinheung variety in 1963, scientists felt that the yield potentials of the japonicas had reached a ceiling, as the yield of this variety was only marginally better than that of the popular Palgeong variety, which was released in 1940. According to U.N. Food and Agriculture Organization statistics, in 1970 the average rice yield in Korea was considerably lower than yields in other temperate rice growing regions (Kim 1979:13).

Spin-offs from the U.S.-Korean military alliance included a considerable amount of economic assistance.[3] Many Korean agricultural scientists received advanced educational training under U.S. Agency for International Development (USAID) auspices. Throughout the 1950s and 1960s United States agricultural scientists worked with Korean academic and government personnel to establish an indigenous agricultural education, research, and extension system. Simultaneously, the International Rice Research Institute (IRRI) began working on a high-yielding rice production technology for the irrigated areas of Asia. By 1965, the short-statured indica, IR-8, was developed and its yield potential widely heralded.[4] The USAID connection in Korea and the involvement of prominent U.S. scientists in IRRI programs facilitated Korean-IRRI cooperation. Korean scientists were sent to IRRI for advanced training in rice breeding and cultivation practices in the 1960s. Several of these IRRI-based Korean scientists, at the direction of ORD, began investigating the possibility of a short-statured indica-japonica cross, an attempt to overcome the yield ceiling that was thought to limit further progress in japonica breeding efforts.

In the fall of 1968, an indica x japonica line was selected (a three-way cross between two indicas—IR-8 and Taichung Native 1—and the japonica Yukara) with yield potential estimated to be 30% higher than the most recently improved japonica releases in Korea. At this time, the ORD Director

General (DG), Kim In Hwan, solicited further IRRI cooperation to accelerate the generational advance of this promising selection and arrange for seed multiplication in the Philippines. The DG remarked: "The cooperative rice breeding program between the Office of Rural Development at Suweon and IRRI will continue with a view to facilitate advancing two to three generations of breeding materials in a single year and expediting the development of improved rice varieties for Korea *in the shortest possible time*" (Kim 1979:19) (emphasis added).

Expectations were established within the highest echelons of the state apparatus (including the president and his staff) that more effective rice production technology existed and that it was imperative to diffuse this new technology as rapidly as possible. The reduction of the varietal development and testing period from the traditional fifteen-seventeen years to six-seven years through a rapid generational advance strategy was the key factor engendering expectations for imminent production increases. The mounting pressures for a "quick fix" rice self-sufficiency solution to Korean agricultural stagnation were expressed in the ORD DG's recollection of a 1968 New Year's Eve meeting with President Park: "I remember vividly the determination of the president on achieving food self-sufficiency, and I decided I would do my best to do it as early as possible" (Kim 1979:21).

By the beginning of 1971 the japonica x indica cross had gone through ten generations and there were plans for countrywide yield trials on 2,750 hectares (ha) at 550 demonstration locations. There was some concern about the palatability of the new variety because of its higher amylose content. The DG related asking officers of ORD and visitors to taste the new variety. Reactions were mixed, but as the Minister of the Economic Planning Board remarked, "Who said palatability of this variety was poor? They must have had full stomachs at the time (Kim 1979:35)." After President Park had tasted the new variety, and graded it good on color and palatability and fair on stickiness, that seemed to settle the question. "Minor" differences in consumption characteristics were not sufficient reasons to sacrifice higher yields promised by the new variety.

The 1971 yield trials went well. Yield increases of 30-40% over the check japonica varieties were registered in experimental plots. The national media ballyhooed the new "miracle" rice. Early in 1972, the new variety was named

Tongil, which means unification in Korean. The new varieties are subsequently referred to by the generic name Tongil. Derivatives of the first Tongil variety were either pureline selections, backcrosses, or crosses closely related to the original germplasm. The important point is that all these new varieties were closely related in a genetic sense.

The success of the 1971 trials secured presidential commitment to the new varieties. ORD had produced enough Tongil seeds to plant 25% of Korean paddy land with the new variety in 1972. Eventually, President Park authorized recommendations for Tongil cultivation on 180,000 ha, approximately 15% of total rice acreage.

The higher yield potential of Tongil was due to its shorter plant height, an increased number of grain-producing spikelets at higher nitrogen fertilization levels, and better light reception because of the erectness of leaves after heading. The idea of designing an optimal plant architecture for photosynthetic efficiency gained wide currency after the IR-8 success at IRRI. This plant type, in addition to exhibiting a more optimal grain/vegetative component ratio and being nitrogen responsive, was good insurance against the frequent late summer typhoons that periodically cause heavy lodging damage on the Korean peninsula. And of perhaps equal significance was the incorporation of genetic resistance to rice blast (from the indica germplasm in the original cross), which had been a perennial source of yield decrease among recommended japonicas.

The major concern about Tongil was its questionable cold tolerance. Indicas are tropical varieties and are classified by agronomists as thermosensitive. The significance of the trait is described as follows:

> Tongil heads early with early transplanting and there is no large variation in the number of days from transplanting to heading whether it is grown in a tropical climate like the Philippines or in a temperate climate like Korea. Therefore, it may be concluded that Tongil is a widely adaptable variety *as long as the temperature is high enough [for it] to grow* (emphasis added). (Kim 1979:50)

According to sources close to the decision, there was much resistance both among administrators in the agrobureaucracy and among scientists within and outside ORD to widespread diffusion of a variety that might be quite susceptible to the fickle Korean climate. However, their objections were overruled at the highest levels, and the go-ahead for dissemination was given to the ORD DG by President Park.

The year 1972 was marked by an unusually cold growing season and cold susceptibility problems emerged. Taste problems have already been mentioned. In addition, the new varieties shattered badly. And an early leaf discoloration—a varietal trait that did not affect yield but worried farmers—also appeared.

Official ORD enthusiasm was not dampened by the Tongil weaknesses. The DG suggested that these problems could be minimized if farmers employed the proper cultural practices. For example, earlier seedbed establishment and transplanting would allow earlier ripening, thus decreasing the possibility of late season, cold temperature damage. If vinyl-covered seedbeds were used to protect young seedlings from the spring cold and irrigation water temperatures were regulated through warming in impoundments, earlier seedbed preparation and transplanting could occur. Transplanting dates would have to be pushed forward to late May in the north and early June in the south. Shattering losses could be minimized with careful threshing techniques in the field. And split applications of nitrogen reduced the leaf discoloration problems and would ease farmers' anxieties. In addition, ORD workers had isolated an earlier maturing Tongil variant suitable for cooler mountainous areas. Work was progressing on improving taste characteristics. In short, official ORD pronouncements were bullish on the new varieties in spite of the problems encountered in 1972. Even a poor crop year produced a reported average yield differential of 20% between Tongil and the traditional varieties (Kim 1979:179).

The cold damage to Tongil was well documented by late 1972. Newspaper accounts of the problems reported that the government blamed unusually heavy rains and fluctuations in temperature for the lower than expected yields. Farmers, however, were claiming that the new varieties were not well adapted to Korean climatic conditions, and some were suggesting that since these new varieties were forced upon them by the government, they should be compensated for losses as a result of involuntary participation in an experiment. There were charges in the press of inadequate experimentation before widespread dissemination.

After the 1972 experience, heated discussions among scientists and administrators about the future of the new variety occurred. The ORD DG pushed for further diffusion from 180,000 ha planted previously to 300,000 ha. Working scientists within ORD were worried about physiological weaknesses, environmental stability problems, and possibilities of pest outbreaks with such wide diffusion of one genotype (recall the considerable diversity over regions in recommended varieties in the late 1960s that provided some protection against monogenetic vulnerability). Ministry of Agriculture officials feared further clamor for damage payments from farmers. And a Japanese consultant group urged gradual diffusion—10,000-20,000 ha expansion per year as a hedge against these uncertainties. Criticisms from the scientific community are recounted by Director General Kim (1979:84):

> Because a significant yield reduction was expected, college professors criticized the susceptibility of Tongil to low temperature, shattering and poor grain quality. Even a college professor who had actively participated in the development of Tongil said that it might be better to recommend the variety *only to farmers who wanted to plant it* (emphasis added).

The Farmer's Role in Varietal Development and Diffusion

What about the farmers who grew the new varieties? Institutionalized, interest group channels for clientele input were nonexistent during the last decade of the Park era. Only if government bureaucrats, extension agents, and researchers, during their visits with farmers and in winter training sessions in the countryside, actively sought out farmers' opinions and expressed them to superiors with decision-making authority would farmers' views be taken into consideration in future discussions about varietal development and diffusion policies. There is little evidence that this sort of feedback occurred on a systematic basis.

Wade (1982:90-91), in his study of irrigation in Korea, is somewhat more positive in his reading of attempts of local government officials to try to articulate the needs of farmer constituents. No evidence of such systematic concern was found in interviews with extension agents and local government officials about the operation of the rice production campaign.

Obviously, the institutional constraints were different. The day-to-day activities of the irrigation associations studied by Wade were somewhat further removed from central government performance pressures that accompany specific national economic development campaigns. In fact, these same associations were pressed into service when Tongil production targets became high profile bureaucratic goals—that is, irrigation association personnel were "requested" to help implement new variety planting targets in their areas of jurisdiction.

Tongil failures were often blamed on farmers' technical incompetence. The ORD DG summarized this position accordingly: "Clearly, many of the problems in growing Tongil could be overcome through improvement of cultural practices. Actually, all the farmers who failed in growing Tongil had made mistakes in managing the variety" (Kim 1979:86)

In the jargon of economists, farmers' objective functions were often different from those of government policymakers. Government policy was to maximize aggregate rice production. Farmers were often more concerned about their own consumption needs and stable yields. It must be remembered that about half of the total rice production was still consumed within the household early in the 1970s (KASS 1972). Thus the much maligned taste of Tongil was an important consideration in production decisions. Rice is the very heart of the Korean diet (from both a physiological and a psychological perspective), and being able to serve high quality rice is an important household consideration in status-conscious Korean society. Many farmers were not willing to sacrifice voluntarily the favored consumption characteristics of traditional varieties for the promise of higher yields for an inferior product.

The government became the purchaser of last resort in order to ensure marketability of the new varieties. Conveniently, government-procured Tongil rice became the staple rations for the 600,000-person Korean military. Soldiers had no choice in the matter, and, thus, it was easy for the government to dispose of a portion of the "unwanted" stocks of the new variety through military procurement channels. In addition, the government inaugurated a dual price policy for rice, whereby the consumer price at sanctioned retail outlets was lower than the purchase price at the farm gate (Shim and Lockwood 1976). In this way, low-income consumers in urban areas were targeted. This "bargain" rice was, of course, Tongil rice.

Activist state intervention in the market did not prevent consumer discrimination due to the perceived lower quality of Tongil varieties. A dual price structure emerged between preferred japonicas and Tongil. Key informants peg the relative price differential at 10-15% during the early 1970s. The most recent NACF (National Agricultural Cooperatives Federation) yearbook quotes price differentials for the period 1976-1984 (with no quotes for the years 1972-75). The average differential for this period was 17% with yearly differentials ranging from 11% to 23% (NACF 1986:52). No varietal price differentials were published in government statistical series throughout the 1970s. Official confirmation of a segmented market would have publicized directly farmer and consumer dissatisfaction with the new varieties. Given the high political visibility of the state's Tongil campaign throughout the period, this statistical omission seems to have been deliberate.

When farmers' adoption responses were weighed from a purely economic perspective, another problem with Tongil was discovered. Due to the potential higher input costs of Tongil production—for example, fertilizer, absolute labor requirements, and more intensive management—it was hard to assess the relative profitability of Tongil over traditional varieties. Especially if one factors in risk considerations that accompany new agronomic practices, farmers were pressed to come up with clear-cut economic criteria for adoption. As yet, there is little published data on farmer varietal selection behavior during the 1970s weighing their perceptions of differential varietal profitability and risk.

Another factor, alluded to earlier, was the difficulty of integrating Tongil into the extant cropping system. Those farmers with rice-barley paddy double-crop systems worked on a tight cropping schedule further aggravated by labor shortages at peak planting and harvesting periods, especially June and October. Moving the rice transplanting dates forward to assure warm weather for critical growth stages made barley cultivation problematic in some areas. Not only was the barley harvest-paddy land preparation and transplanting timetable further compressed, but an early barley harvest raised questions about substantial yield decreases due to a shortened maturity period. Also, farmers who planted early spring crops, such as vegetables and melons, in paddy land preceding the summer rice crop could not adjust easily to the Tongil varieties. Japonicas could be transplanted later in a spring vegetable-rice crop rotation scheme and still produce what many farmers considered to be an adequate harvest given their double-cropping preferences. Although ORD officially denied adverse impact on cropping systems, this position was not articulated by key informants. That Tongil was out of synchronization with widely practiced cropping systems was acknowledged by everyone to whom the question was put. Interviews with farmers about how they managed double cropping further corroborated this view.

Furthermore, it could be argued that the Tongil route to rice self-sufficiency led to decreased *aggregate* food self-sufficiency due to interference with previous cropping system patterns. ORD program pronouncements tended to speak of rice and food self-sufficiency goals interchangeably due to the predominance of rice in Korea's staple foodgrain mix, but it appeared that the Tongil drive inadvertently discouraged double cropping. It is difficult to separate the effects of the technical constraints of Tongil cultivation from other intervening market factors (product and labor market) that are probable causes of double-cropping acreage decline, especially declines in the traditional winter cereals (barley and wheat) grown on paddy land. Nevertheless, the pressures for Tongil adoption seemed often to conflict with attempts to maximize land utilization through intensified cropping strategies. At present, the land constraint in Korea is, of course, a key factor limiting agricultural adjustment. Once again, rural-urban income differentials are widening due in part to lagging relative productivity trends in agriculture. The Tongil program, in other words, may have contributed to subsequent sectoral adjustment problems in the economy.[5]

If there were so many questions lingering about Tongil adaptability and profitability, how then did the government manage to convince farmers to plant a considerable portion of Korean rice paddy acreage to the new variety during the diffusion campaign? Again, this question was quite sensitive politically, so the historical evidence is scanty. It appears that areas initially thought suitable for the new varieties were chosen through soil survey analysis data and that this information was passed down to local administrators for whom planting targets were prescribed. Rural guidance (extension) agents were given the unenviable task of "convincing" farmers to plant the new variety. These acreage targets were taken seriously by local officials. The promotion of the county administrator to a more attractive position (preferably near a large city) depends on his jurisdiction's performance in achieving plan targets sent down from central government and provincial offices.

Varied strategies were used to gain compliance. The ORD DG captured the most common method in this observation: "In Sinan-gun, Jeonnam-do guidance workers persuaded farmers to plant Tongil under the slogan of 'Visit Farmers Ten Times.' Many farmers accepted the recommendation to save the guidance worker's 'face'" (Kim 1979:87). This mode of reaching agreement by pestering the opposition into stolid consent is apparently a time-honored modus operandi in the Korean bureaucratic setting (Aqua 1974). More heavy-handed measures were also taken. Government-supplied inputs such as fertilizer were often used to coax compliance. And, in interviews with farmers, confirmation was found of the allegation that, as a last resort, traditional variety seedbeds were physically destroyed by rural guidance workers and other responsible local officials.

The dense agrobureaucracy was mobilized in support of Tongil adoption. When interviewing at the county administrative level in South Kyeongsang province in the summer of 1982, the author was given a rather blunt written description of agricultural adjustments during the Tongil promotion campaign in the 1970s. According to this document, the degree of official cajoling and monitoring was so intense that farmers started to refer to specific rice seedbeds and areas designated for new variety production as the county magistrate's plot, the chief of police's plot, etc. This type of official penetration into everyday affairs at the county and township levels, a legacy of Japanese colonial rule, is extremely intense by third world standards.

Reed's (1979) fieldwork on government-sponsored organizational means of penetration to achieve Tongil diffusion targets captured a corporate, organizational type of state intervention. Due to the more intensive management required for Tongil establishment and maintenance—covered seedbeds, more careful water management, vigilant pest monitoring and increasing pesticide applications, and more careful harvesting and threshing—the government promoted group farming schemes to encourage proper cultural practices. Prospective joint farming areas were identified by rural guidance officers. After much "persuading," some critical operations were undertaken by these groups in order to ensure proper Tongil cultivation practices. Reed questioned the viability of this joint farming approach both in terms of the top-down methods used in organizing the farmers into cooperative work teams and the long-term sustainability of the effort given the apparent instability of the technology.

Farmers' preferences, it appears, were neglected in the Tongil campaign. It was an economic and political penetration scheme launched from above. National priorities, as dictated by officials of the state, not aggregated individual preferences, were the motivating force behind the Tongil development and diffusion campaign.

The Rise and Fall of Tongil

After the problematic 1972 experience with Tongil, the 1973 diffusion targets were the subject of heated controversy within the agrobureaucracy. Administrators in the Ministry of Agriculture and scientists (especially academics outside ORD) cautioned against further promotion of the new variety due to questions about its adaptability to the vagaries of Korean climate and because of farmer opposition. In December, 1972, a food production planning board established by President Park reemphasized the rice self-sufficiency goal. The ORD DG, seeing Tongil as the only readily available means to this end, pushed for further Tongil diffusion in spite of what he perceived as active opposition within the Ministry of Agriculture. The provincial ORDs were directed to encourage Tongil production in "appropriate fields within the adapted regions" (Kim 1979:87). As mentioned earlier, it was the ORD position that better management practices would solve the problems encountered in the previous year. Although the eventual acreage planted with Tongil in 1973 was much below Kim's target of 300,000 ha (140,000 ha were actually planted), the weather was favorable. The average yield for Tongil was estimated to be over 30% higher than traditional japonica yields (Kim 1979:92). In August, 1973, a new Minister of Agriculture was appointed who sided with the ORD DG on Tongil diffusion policy. The outlook for Tongil brightened considerably, and plans were made to disseminate the new varieties over a wider area in the years ahead.

The Tongil diffusion push continued in the wake of an auspicious 1973 crop. Table 4-1 indicates the trends in new variety acreage and yield. Table 4-2 shows that improvements in Tongil lines came rapidly on stream. Rice breeders had

TABLE 4-1. Rice Variety and Production Data (1970-1983)

Year	(1) Tongil Adoption (% Acreage)	(2) Yield Comparisons Tongils (MT/ha)	Traditional (MT/ha)	(3) Total Production (Million MT)
1970	0	---	3.3	3.94
1971	0	---	3.4	4.00
1972	16(9)[a]	3.9	3.2	3.98
1973	10(7)[a]	4.8	3.4	4.23
1974	15	4.7	3.5	4.42
1975	23	5.0	3.5	4.63
1976	44	4.8	4.0	5.18
1977	54	5.5	4.2	5.97
1978	85(76)[a]	4.9	4.4	5.78
1979	61	4.6	4.4	5.46
1980	50	---	---	3.60
1981	27	---	---	4.92
1982	33	---	---	5.12
1983	34	---	---	5.33

[a]Data in parenthesis is taken from Dalrymple (1985:100).

Note: Unfortunately, we have not been able to obtain comparative Tongil-traditional variety yield data for the years 1980-83. However, it is reported in "The Rice Production Policy of the Republic of Korea," International Rice Commission Newsletter (December, 1982, p. 17) that Tongil-type varieties must yield 15-25% higher than traditional varieties for farmers to find them more profitable. From 1978 to 1983, Tongil-type varietal yields are estimated to have been only 9.4% higher than traditional variety yields. (This reference is cited in Dalrymple (1985)).

Sources: Crill, Ham and Beachell (1982, Table 1). Data is taken from official Korean Ministry of Agriculture and Fisheries (MAF) statistical series.

TABLE 4-2. Diffusion Patterns of Tongil and Tongil-Type Varieties (1976-1978)

	Total Tongil Acreage (%)		
Variety	1976	1977	1978
Yushin	0.6	57.9	35.4
Tongil	96.3	26.5	10.5
Tongil (early)	1.3	9.0	9.7
Yeongnam (early)	1.5	4.4	3.3
Milyang 22	0.0	1.3	7.1
Tongil glutinous	0.4	0.5	1.4
Milyang 21	0.0	0.2	18.4
Milyang 23	0.0	0.1	12.5
Others	0.0	0.0	1.7

Source: Dalrymple (1980, Table 25)

succeeded in developing shorter maturity variants for northern and mountainous areas, hopefully providing more protection against cold temperature vulnerability. Several variants showed markedly improved palatability characteristics. Some favorable disease and insect resistance traits were also incorporated. This package of improvements led ORD officials to believe that rapid progress was being made with the green revolution.

The euphoria over rice production accomplishments reached its zenith at a New Year's news conference in 1977 when President Park announced that South Korea, on humanitarian grounds, was ready to extend food aid to North Korea, which reportedly suffered from food shortages due to a bad harvest in the preceding year (Kihl 1979:142). The South, in contrast, had achieved its vaunted goal of supplying all its rice consumption needs through the Tongil effort. Rice self-sufficiency had become a productive asset in the international rivalry between the North and South.

Progress came to a halt in 1978 with a nationwide blast outbreak among the widely disseminated Tongils. Previously, these varieties had been resistant to blast. But resistance was apparently located in a single major gene source that finally broke down. Simultaneously, due to the epidemiological dynamics of the mutated blast pathogen on susceptible Tongils, which were now spread throughout the country, the population of races attacking the japonicas declined. This change increased the advantages of japonica over Tongil cultivation with respect to the risk of blast damage. In 1979, more problems occurred with disease susceptibility and wind and rain damage. But the 1980 crop year brought disaster. Cold weather similar to that experienced in 1972 caused widespread crop failures, which resulted in an overall decline of 30% in rice production. The new Chun government, fearing panic about a rice shortage in an already precarious political environment, scurried to purchase rice from any available source.[6] The consequences of the 1980 Tongil episode for new variety acreage in subsequent years are shown in Table 4-1.

Although many government and ORD officials attributed the Tongil failure to God's will, a debate over the wisdom of the Tongil diffusion strategy could not be avoided.[7] Charges were levelled about lack of proper regional testing over extant environmental variations, the critical lack of cold tolerance in these varieties, and the diffusion of a monogenetic rice culture. The credibility of the government extension service was seriously compromised. After the 1980 disaster, past government varietal recommendation policy was difficult to justify to farmers, and edicts coming down to local county and township officials about what varieties to recommend to achieve production targets were contradictory. At one point in 1981, the Ministry of Agriculture sent down the word that farmers could select their own varieties. Later, the message was that farmers should be encouraged to plant a 50/50 Tongil-japonica mix in order to assure that government production targets were met. Extension agent informants in South Kyeongsang province told the author that the government was allowing farmers freedom of choice in varietal selection during the 1982 crop season in response to farmer dissatisfaction with Tongil performance. Dalrymple (1986:52) reports that final government authorization of freedom of choice relating to varietal selection occurred in 1984.

This discussion does not imply, of course, that comparable varietal breakdowns do not occur when agricultural research programs are more responsive to societal demands. Modern monocrop agriculture relies on the continual modification of varieties to keep ahead of mutating pathogens. The problem in this case was that the government's heavy-handed varietal diffusion campaign magnified the social and political fallout from a technology breakdown. Panic in the agrobureaucracy and farmer resistance to future innovations is likely to be reduced in a sociopolitical context where technology adoption is perceived by researchers, extension agents, and clients alike as a voluntary response to a range of possible technical options.

The emphasis on the Tongil rice-breeding strategy can only be understood in light of the yield maximization goals articulated at the highest levels of the Korean polity. The top-down political pressures for quick results mitigated against adjustments in the breeding program. For example, the introduction of cold tolerance characteristics from japonica germplasm threatened to modify the ideal plant type upon which Tongil high yield characteristics were based. As one informant emphasized, it was very difficult for information about production problems or trends at the farm level to be filtered up through the bureaucratic decision-making ranks without the information being distorted to fit preconceived notions supporting previously approved strategies to achieve government goals.

This problem is well illustrated by trends in on-farm yield differentials between Tongil and japonica varieties during the 1970s (see Table 4-1). Due to farmers' ongoing experience with cold tolerance problems and increasing disease susceptibility in the Tongils, they applied less fertilizer than required for maximum production under optimal environmental conditions. This was certainly an economic response to risk factors inherent in the variety coupled with increases in fertilizer prices due to a sharp rise in the cost of imported oil. At the same time, many of the cultural practices for Tongil production were equally effective in raising japonica output. And given the price differentials between varieties, farmers were tending the marketed japonicas with more care. These on-the-farm responses to a combination of technical and market forces were altering further the previously questionable economic margin of Tongils over japonicas. A recent analysis suggests that Tongil yield increases of 15-25% over traditional varieties were required to assure Tongil economic advantage (Dalrymple 1986). Tongil yield differentials averaged only 9.4% over the period 1978-1983 (Dalrymple 1986:94).

During the decade of the 1970s, there is no evidence that sustained efforts were made to improve extant japonicas, especially with regard to disease resistance where considerable progress appeared possible through backcrossing with disease-resistant indica strains. There is disagreement among scientists in Korea about the genetic potential for japonica yield improvement. However, it is acknowledged by most scientists to whom we put the question that the japonica breeding effort was relegated to a maintenance operation during this period. The one-track road to increased rice production—the Tongil route—was the focus of all serious breeding efforts. When the Tongil varieties deteriorated, the government was faced with a serious dilemma. Officials lacked an alternative technology to push at that critical point. The previously mentioned confusion over varietal recommendation policies resulted from Tongil overkill.

The Korean Green Revolution and the Developmental State

The conventional wisdom about the introduction of new improved agricultural technologies is that their development requires close attention to location specific adaptation. One of the most important roles of the agricultural scientist is to test new technologies under realistic conditions—that is, conditions that reflect both expected environmental variability and farm conditions. The scientist, if he/she is properly trained and given adequate resources, will develop feasible production improvements. And, so the story goes, farmers will gradually adopt production improvements that are adapted to their resource base and that correspond to their preference schedules. If one accepts the conventional wisdom, the paradox of the Korean green revolution is that new rice varieties were developed and diffused quickly in the face of disputes within the scientific community about their viability and in the face of farmer responses that were ambivalent at best.

The most striking characteristic of the varietal development campaign was the dedication of those at the apex of the agrobureaucracy to spread new varieties with promising yield traits as rapidly as possible. The campaign was similar to economic development pushes in other sectors—that is, targets were set and timetables established for their completion.

This case—in which high-yielding varieties were widely adopted by Korean farmers in spite of opposition to aspects of the program by scientists and farmers alike—confounds recent "society-centered" interpretations of agricultural research system activities. Rather than being a case of a "well-articulated" research program in the induced innovation mode—that is, a program effected through close cooperation between government officials, researchers, extension agents, and farmers (Evenson, Waggoner, and Ruttan 1979)—the South Korean green revolution was an effort by the developmental state to achieve strategic production goals through a combination of what Dahl and Lindblom (1953) call field manipulation and command strategies (Jones and Sakong 1980:80-84). The homogeneity of Korean agriculture facilitated the rapid spread and initial success of the Tongil program in terms of aggregate production increases, but eventually this blunt instrument was thwarted by the ever-present ecological changes in agricultural systems.

Heretofore, this analysis of "green revolution" agricultural research activities has been extracted from the broader contexts of rural and national development policy. By bringing these larger agendas back into the analysis, the rice varietal development drive is put into strategic perspective. In fact, the varietal development program was only one component of a policy package designed to effect rice self-sufficiency. Rice self-sufficiency, in turn, was an integral component of the overall industrialization program (Burmeister 1987b). Not only were technological improvements (principally, the new varieties) emphasized, but production incentives such as higher rice prices and cheap fertilizer were promulgated. A shift in terms of trade favorable to agriculture, a shift which rarely occurs in countries at comparable levels of development, was implemented. These trends are shown below in Table 4-3. In addition, as mentioned previously, government purchasing and marketing of "inferior" rice was intensified to facilitate the Tongil production drive. Government purchasing trends are revealed below in Table 4-4. This policy package was capped in 1971 with the inauguration of the New Community Movement (NCM, or *Saemaul Undong* in Korean)—a massive political penetration effort designed to secure continued support for the Park regime through a variety of infrastructural improvement measures aimed at boosting rural living standards (Ban, Moon, and Perkins 1980:275-280; Lee 1981; Brandt and Lee 1981). Increasing crop production was seen an important means to NCM goals of rural development. The amount of political resources put into this effort at all administrative levels shows the extent to which the initiatives came from the president and his top aides (Park 1981). Separate NCM bureaus were appended to township and county administrative offices to ensure that NCM targets were taken seriously.

TABLE 4-3. Rice Prices (1962-1979)

Year	(1) Gov't Purchase Price (Current Won/80 kg)	(2) Adjusted Purchase Price (Adjusted Won/80 kg)[a]	(3) Nominal Protection Rate (Percent)[b]	(4) Rice/fertilizer Price Ratio (100-1 bag rice/ 25 kg urea)
1962	1,650	12,692	-34	4.33
1963	2,060	13,919	22	7.03
1964	2,967	15,782	27	7.16
1965	3,150	12,550	-5	4.69
1966	3,306	11,765	-6	4.94
1967	3,590	11,848	1	6.49
1968	4,200	12,389	14	7.54
1969	5,150	13,273	24	8.39
1970	7,000	15,873	30	8.97
1971	8,750	17,570	84	11.27
1972	9,888	17,532	126	14.18
1973	11,377	18,469	27	13.29
1974	15,760	19,481	7	14.36
1975	19,500	19,500	19	10.79
1976	23,200	18,573	121	7.35
1977	26,260	17,962	193	8.13
1978	30,000	15,781	229	9.53
1979	36,600	16,929	240	12.16

[a] Calculated in constant won (1975 = base year).

[b] Nominal rate of protection represents the percentage deviation of domestic prices from international market prices for rice. Positive values indicate that domestic prices are higher than international prices.

Sources: Columns 1-3 are taken from Kim and Joo (1982, Table 3-2, p. 38 and Table 4-9, p. 84). Column 4 is taken from Burmeister (1985, Table 33, p. 280).

After years of neglect, why the sudden shift to production promotion policies—including the new varietal development and diffusion campaign—motivated by the highly publicized target of rice self-sufficiency? One must examine the domestic political position of the Park regime, the relative power of the state at this time over industrial and rural interests, the potential contributions of increased agricultural production to the national economic development project, and changes in the international context (both economic and political) which,

TABLE 4-4. Marketing of Rice through Government Channels (1970-1983)

Year	Percentage[a]	Year	Percentage
1970	.09	1977	.23
1971	.13	1978	.23
1972	.13	1979	.23
1973	.12	1980	.15
1974	.17	1981	.18
1975	.17	1982	.21
1976	.20	1983	.23

[a] Percentage of total rice production marketed through the National Agricultural Cooperatives Federation. During this period, approximately 50% of total Korean rice production passed through market channels (government and private).

Source: National Agricultural Cooperatives Federation (various years).

according to the rationale of state officials, made a change in policy necessary in order to cope more effectively with both the internal strains and external constraints of latecomer industrialization.

Throughout the 1950s and 1960s, low grain price policies were adopted as a means of surplus extraction and political control. The state was, in effect, engaged in forming an export-oriented entrepreneurial class that was competitive in world markets. Keeping wage costs low facilitated this economic development strategy. In addition, low food prices helped to diffuse potential urban unrest. The influx of rural migrants into the cities, especially Seoul, posed an omnipresent threat to the political order. Control over the prices of essential foodstuffs became a policy tool with which to manage potentially restless urban marginal classes.

Price-induced shortfalls in foodgrain production and marketing were met by grants from the United States Public Law (PL) 480 program. Staple foodgrains were provided to Korea on concessionary terms during the 1950s and 1960s. Low foodgrain price policies were reinforced by the dumping of significant amounts of U.S. surplus rice, barley, and wheat on the Korean market. The foreign aid dependent Rhee regime became addicted to this flow of U.S. commodities, as recurrent government expenditures were financed, in part, from local currency sales of the PL 480 stocks.

By the end of the 1960s, the United States had started to withdraw PL 480 support from South Korea. This change in policy reflected the deteriorating international economic position of the United States. Increasing balance of payments problems and dollar support crises led to the 1971 decision to scrap fixed exchange rates. In effect, the United States acknowledged the gradual erosion of its postwar economic hegemony. The export earning potential of United States agriculture was increasingly emphasized by the Nixon administration. Thus, hard currency sales were encouraged, and countries like South Korea that were felt to have progressed economically were asked to pay their own way.

The shock of the PL 480 withdrawals could be handled by Korean state officials in two ways. Either imports could be purchased with foreign exchange at world market prices, or increased agricultural production could be promoted to try to close the gap. Increased agricultural production required not only improved production technology, but also price incentives. The state, at this time, was in an especially good bargaining position vis-à-vis the interests, especially industry, to opt for the latter strategy. While the cost of wage goods for exporters might be increased by a foodgrains import substitution policy, these businesses were financed primarily through loan capital which was channeled through state banks (Cole and Park 1983). Strong opposition to government policy might adversely affect access to credit, which was necessary for both operating expenses and expansion in highly leveraged Korean firms. In addition, much business expansion depended on the availability of foreign exchange for capital goods and intermediate inputs. Business growth prospects would be dampened by the diversion of foreign exchange to food imports. Finally, export markets in the industrialized nations are sensitive to quality differentials. Export-oriented Korean entrepreneurs realized that domestic market expansion provided a valuable buffer against the rigors of international competition—in other words, gradual quality improvements could be developed at the expense of captive domestic consumers. Putting more income into the hands of a large rural population through a foodgrains import substitution policy created domestic demand for Korea's nascent consumer goods industries. Important "carrots" were thus balanced against the "stick" of wage goods increases in the fashioning of the foodgrains import substitution policy package. Wage goods increases, in turn, were moderated somewhat by the dual price structure for government-purchased rice and barley (Kim and Joo 1982:43) which, in effect, subsidized basic food staples for low-income consumers.

President Park and his political advisors saw gains from a rice self-sufficiency policy package. Agricultural sector neglect was increasingly worrisome to those concerned with the regime's political legitimacy, which was based almost exclusively on the ability to improve living standards through rapid industrialization policies. By the late 1960s, increasing rural-urban income disparities threatened to erode Park's base of political support in the countryside. It is rumored that a Korean CIA study of rural areas in the late 1960s warned of increasing resentment against the discriminatory development policies targeted exclusively to favored industrial sectors and/or regions of the country. The KASS (1972) report estimated that in 1971 rural per capita income was 33% of urban figures. Opposition politicians campaigned against the increasing sectoral and regional income disparities (this was before the imposition of martial law and the promulgation of the Yushin constitution in 1972, which drastically limited political activities not sponsored by the Park political organization). The potential danger to plebiscitary approval became apparent when Park lost the agricultural southwestern provinces to Kim Dae-Jung in Korea's last contested election in 1971. The government party had always counted on a secure rural support base to counter its traditional electoral difficulties in urban districts.

The importance of rice in the crop mix of the average Korean farmer made a rice self-sufficiency production campaign centered on new high-yielding varieties, when coupled with price support and input subsidy measures, an attractive income policy for rural areas. In fact, Adelman and Robinson (1978:191), using Korean data to test a macroeconomic model of income distribution consequences of various policy interventions, showed that the one program that made the most difference in moving toward a more equitable distribution outcome was increasing the terms of trade for agriculture. Reduction of the rural-urban income gap during the 1970s is a widely cited consequence of increased rice production and higher prices for rice (Ban, Moon, and Perkins 1980, Ch. 11; Lee 1979).

The importance of this rice production strategy in

minimizing further regional disparities was strikingly illustrated in Keidel's (1981) work on regional production and income trends in Korean agriculture. Improvements in the transportation system brought increased incomes to upland areas and other locales once regarded as marginal agricultural production regions when compared to the southwestern rice bowl provinces. Increasing disposable incomes of urbanites had altered farm commodity demand patterns. Vegetables, fruit, and livestock products with higher income elasticities of demand could be produced in these formerly marginal regions. Due to their proximity to the transportation arteries to Seoul and Pusan, they enjoyed a comparative advantage in marketing, and farm incomes increased relative to other regions. The regions outside this transportation network—regions that had been discriminated against in industrial development policies and thus were more dependent on farm income (the politically volatile southwest provinces)—would have suffered a further shock in relative income position if the old rice production and price policies had remained in effect. Thus, the supply promotion strategy helped to meliorate increasing regional income disparities at a time of increasing regional tensions.

The military coup in 1961 greatly strengthened the linkages between the executive branch of the government and the national security apparatus (Kim 1978). One might even argue that these two state bureaucracies were fused as a result of the coup. Thus the preferences of this bureaucratic faction weigh heavily in intrastate bargaining over policy. The national security officials were undoubtedly willing to sacrifice some economic efficiency goals to promote a rice self-sufficiency campaign that would not only diffuse domestic political unrest by effecting some redistribution of income but could also be justified as a national defense measure in the North-South conflict.

The unravelling of the U.S. position in Southeast Asia and the unsettling recognition of the People's Republic of China at the expense of formal relations with Taiwan (and what that implied for United States defense and aid commitments) undoubtedly strengthened the hands of those within the state who supported aggressive agricultural production policies. Instabilities in the world grain markets accompanying the Russian grain sale and the subsequent U.S. embargo showed clearly the risks of becoming overly reliant on grain imports. This self-reliance policy theme was clearly evident in accounts of important economic policy decisions in the late 1970s supporting a crash, heavy industry development program (Kim 1980). As in the case of most policy rationalizations in South Korea, high ranking state officials shifted the terms of public discussion from who gained and lost to the global imperative of national survival. Self-sufficiency in a hostile, undependable world was a frequently voiced economic policy preference among national security officials.

Finally, increased food self-sufficiency, as noted earlier in President Park's offer of food aid to North Korea, was used as a weapon in the international propaganda war between the North and the South. North Korea has made much of its self-reliant national development strategy designed to prevent foreign exploitation. They have long claimed to be self-sufficient in foodstuffs. In the international jockeying among the Koreas, the propaganda impact of claiming a food production revolution has not been lost on South Korean officials. The emphasis placed on training programs for other third world crop production and extension specialists in rice production technology now given by ORD is a concrete expression of the international diplomatic utility of South Korean accomplishments in agriculture.

The paradox of the Korean green revolution—that a new technology could be rapidly diffused in the face of widespread scientific doubts and producer opposition—lies in the elevation of the campaign to a highly articulated national goal. No clearer evidence of this can be cited than the naming of the new varietal type. As stated previously, Tongil means unification in Korean. If there is any overriding political theme in South Korea's postwar history, it is a steadfast commitment to the ideal of the eventual reunification of the two Koreas. The symbolic force of this idea—the fact that the culturally homogeneous Korean peninsula has been perceived as one political and social unit throughout modern history and that these ties are even more acutely felt due to the personal dislocation and familial separation accompanying partition—has been powerful enough to legitimate various draconian measures taken in the name of eventual reunification by repressive regimes in both the North and the South. Officials of the South Korean state effectively played on these collective emotions in their attempt to meet rice production targets.

The rice production goals were attempts to deal with exigencies faced by state officials who were charting a national development course amidst political and economic pressures of both international and domestic origin. The historical evolution of the state/society relationship in South Korea did not produce organized private sector interests, such as those envisioned in the society-centered models of public policy, which exert countervailing pressures and are able to initiate programs funded by state agencies. Rather, the story of the Korean green revolution reveals a developmental state whose top policymakers decided how agricultural sector targets were to be met and had the policy and organizational instruments at their disposal to carry out their programs even if the programs did not correspond to the preferences of important societal interests.

In Chapter 5, we see how state preferences were articulated in the allocation of funds and personnel to different agricultural research activities in the Office of Rural Development.

Notes

1. Information in this chapter is drawn from two principal sources—key informant interviews with government-employed agricultural scientists, university scientists, local government officials, extension agents, and farmers and the memoirs of former ORD Director General Kim In Hwan (1979). Since opinions expressed by key informants are sometimes at variance with the official government interpretation of the Korean agricultural development experience, anonymity of informants has been preserved at the author's discretion. Further information about key informants may be obtained upon request. The frequent citations from Dr. Kim's memoirs illustrate the institutional context of agricultural research decision making in Korea. In no way are they intended as personal criticisms of Dr. Kim. During his tenure as ORD Director General, his personal dedication to the improvement of Korean agriculture was highly respected.

2. See Barker and Herdt (1985, Ch. 2) for a detailed explanation of the biological differences between indica and japonica rice cultivars.

3. Steinberg (1985) summarizes the dimensions and impact of U.S. economic assistance to Korea.

4. Indica varieties are tropical rice types with different

plant archetypes, temperature tolerances, and photoperiod sensitivity characteristics (essentially insensitive to daylength).

5. More information about cropping systems in Korea may be found in Desrosiers, Kopf, and Yohe (1978:41-49).

6. In October, 1979, President Park was assassinated by the director of the Korean CIA. In December, 1979, General Chun took control of the country in a military coup in which a civil war among contending military factions was narrowly averted. In May, 1980, an insurrection in Kwangju protesting the Chun usurpation of power was brutally suppressed by special military units. The definitive history of these events has yet to appear for obvious political reasons.

7. In fairness to the Tongil proponents, it must be acknowledged that japonica yields were also well below normal due to unseasonably cool growing conditions during pollination, grain-filling, and ripening stages. It is widely admitted, however, that japonica yields were less adversely affected. This varietal type seems more stable under Korean climatic conditions.

5
Research Priorities: State Power or Market Power?

Questions about the responsiveness of agricultural research policy to societal interests are often addressed by looking at patterns of agricultural research expenditures. The distribution of agricultural research budgets across commodities and regions reveals research priorities. The material and informational outputs of the agricultural research system are conditioned by the allocation of resources to particular research activities. The outputs, in turn, define which social groups are most likely to benefit from agricultural research programs. In this chapter, questions about the social responsiveness and accountability of the Korean agricultural research system are addressed via the analysis of research resource allocation. This information is useful in charting the relative import of market power and state power in the determination of research priorities and the direction of technical change in agriculture.

Three types of information are reviewed in this chapter. First, Korean agricultural research budget allocations are analyzed in comparative perspective. Second, the material outputs of the Korean agricultural research system are catalogued. Third, two brief case studies of the bureaucratic logic behind research initiatives are used to illustrate how state preferences often determine what is done.

Korean Agricultural Research Budget Allocations in Comparative Perspective

A robust literature has developed around the problem of resource allocation in agricultural research (Ruttan 1982, Chs.

10, 11). Several factors account for this interest. Studies of agricultural productivity growth (the decreasing ratio of inputs to output) point to the catalytic role of agricultural research investments. Not only are significant productivity gains attributed to research, but the cost effectiveness of these research investments is claimed to be quite high relative to other infrastructural investments. Because a significant portion of agricultural research activities are funded by the public sector, questions about accountability—who benefits from research programs—adds a political dimension to the discussion of the research resource allocation problem.

For the problem at hand, it is useful to disaggregate the agricultural research budget by commodity expenditures. These commodity-specific funding allocations are then compared to economic indicators of commodity value to determine the fit between budgetary allocations and the economic importance of the commodity. This fit indicates potential social payoffs from a portfolio of agricultural research projects. An efficient agricultural research system maximizes these payoffs. The level of economic benefits associated with technical innovations in agriculture is likely to be correlated with the value of the affected commodity. Commodity values, in turn, are said to measure social preferences; on the demand side prices reveal consumer wants, on the supply side commodities offered reveal producer choices among production alternatives.

Agricultural economists have put forth a "parity" model of research resource allocation as a first approximation of a research policy outcome that is congruent with social welfare maximization. It is readily acknowledged that the parity model is flawed. The model assumes that "the opportunities for productive scientific effort or productivity-enhancing technical change are equivalent in each commodity and resource category" and "that the value of a scientific or technical innovation is proportional to the value of the commodity or the value of the contribution of a particular resource to production" (Ruttan 1982:265). These caveats notwithstanding, Boyce and Evenson (1975) argue that an index of the congruence between research resource allocation and commodity value reflects the relative efficiency of an agricultural research system and its responsiveness to its prime clients, producers and consumers of agricultural products. A research-commodity congruity index was developed by Boyce and Evenson (1975:14-15) to analyze research resource allocation patterns by commodity or region.

The index is calculated in the following way:

$$\text{Congruence} = 1 - \text{Sum}(C_i - R_i)^2$$

where C_i = Share of the ith commodity or region in total agricultural value product
R_i = Share of research expenditure in the ith commodity or region

If research resource allocations (percentages of total research expenditures allocated to particular commodities or regions) are matched perfectly with the economic weights of commodities or regions (percentages of total value of agricultural production), the index will equal unity. The distance from unity indicates the extent of "mismatching" between the research enterprise and the social value of agricultural activities. After calculating research-commodity congruity indices for a cross section of countries grouped by per capita income levels at specified points in time, Boyce and Evenson (1975:96) concluded, "It cannot automatically be assumed that perfect congruity represents optimality. Nonetheless, it would appear that as research systems expand and mature they move toward congruity. Accordingly, it is probably the case that this index is closely related to efficiency."

In order to interpret Korean patterns of research expenditures, comparative reference points are necessary. Table 5-1 shows research-commodity congruity indices for a sample of developing countries. These indices have been calculated by Judd, Boyce, and Evenson (1983). In an earlier publication, Boyce and Evenson (1975:94, 96) noted patterns of consistency between congruity index values. "Low-income" countries tended to exhibit lower values on the research-commodity congruity index. Several possibilities were cited as probable causes for this pattern. First, the colonial legacies of many of these countries left agricultural research systems heavily weighted toward those export commodities of most interest to the metropole. Ruttan's (1982:100-107) case study of the evolution of Malaysian agricultural research capacity is illustrative of this tendency. During the colonial era rubber was accorded priority over other commodities in British-controlled Malaya. Only after independence did a more balanced commodity research mix evolve. Second, ecological variation is pronounced in many of

TABLE 5-1. Cross-National Comparison of Research-Commodity Congruity Indices

Country/Region	Congruity Index Average 1972-75	Congruity Index Average 1976-79
Africa		
Egypt	.905	.939
Ghana	.906	.912
Kenya	.861	.840
Nigeria	.668	.675
Sudan	.888	.900
Tanzania	.763	.747
Tunisia	.892	.938
Uganda	.733	.826
Asia		
Bangladesh	.675	.716
India	.935	.912
Indonesia	.816	.878
Korea (South)	.908	.842
Malaysia	.662	.534
Pakistan	.909	.949
Philippines	.404	.574
Sri Lanka	.731	.666
Taiwan	.957	.980
Thailand	.919	.927
Turkey	.957	.908
Latin America		
Argentina	.962	.982
Brazil	.963	.982
Chile	.910	.950
Colombia	.968	.933
Mexico	.884	.854
Peru	.954	.938
Venezuela	.946	.874

Source: Judd, Boyce, and Evenson (1983, Table 11, p. 27).

the tropical and semitropical countries. The potential for resource "misallocation" (indicated by low values on research-commodity congruity indices) is partly a function of ecological variability. This problem has been compounded by the historical neglect of agricultural research in tropical and semitropical food staples such as cassava, sweet potatoes, and millet (Judd, Boyce, and Evenson 1986:92). Obviously, the new nations must draw on an extant stock of scientific knowledge during the formative stages of research system development. The knowledge base for relevant research in certain crops may be lacking. Finally, ineffective political articulation between the end-users and/or producers of agricultural commodities and agricultural researchers in the new nations is a possible explanation for lower research-commodity congruity indices.

As stated earlier, congruence does not always represent an optimal allocation of resources. For example, Boyce and Evenson (1975:94) remark that "perfect congruence will not be ideal when international trade is taken into account. Optimal investment would require a bias toward heavily traded commodities because of high demand elasticities." In aggregate terms, benefits from agricultural research are maximized when trading opportunities are optimized. However, the politics of productivity increases complicate any simple calculation based on aggregate gains from trade. Relative gains to producers and consumers (both domestic and foreign) depend on market structure (Ruttan 1982:270-271). For example, in a small trading country, production increases are likely to have little impact on world prices. Productivity gains are thus likely to accrue to producers. In a large trading country that supplies a considerable proportion of the world market in a particular commodity, productivity increases may lower world prices. Productivity gains then accrue mainly to domestic and foreign consumers. Further complications occur under various regimes of agricultural protection. The main point is that agricultural research benefits are filtered through market power and social power prisms. An aggregate social welfare function, so often posited in estimating the benefits of agricultural research, is based on extant distributions of assets and market shares.

Table 5-1 provides interesting cross-national comparisons. Countries with long histories of strong export performance in industrial and nonstaple food crops—Nigeria, Malaysia, Philippines, Sri Lanka—have low congruity indices, suggesting a continuing emphasis in research programs on increasing export crop productivity. India and Indonesia, with large domestic markets for basic food staples and rapidly growing populations, have much higher congruity ratios even though historically they have also had strong nonfood primary product export sectors. And the highest ratios are found in countries whose agricultural policies have been supportive of both domestic staple and export commodities (Taiwan) and/or countries where strong domestic demand and demand for export production coincide (Pakistani cotton and wheat and Thai rice).

How should the Korean research-commodity congruity indices be interpreted in comparative perspective? There are important characteristics of Korean agriculture that place a priori constraints on possibilities for low congruity index values. First, Korea does not have a large agricultural export sector. The country has not exported appreciable amounts of agricultural produce since liberation from Japanese colonial rule in 1945. And, significantly, research and export emphasis during the colonial period was focused on the preferred staple foodgrain, rice. The second major factor is the homogeneity of Korean agriculture. Korea is a small country and, for all practical purposes, can be treated as an ecological unit when compared to many larger nations with diverse ecotypes. Lack of ecological diversity limits variations in cropping systems. As noted previously, the less variation in an agricultural system, the less chance of misallocation of research resources across commodities. Homogeneity is also evident with regard to the size of operational holding. Recalling discussions in Chapter 3 about land reform and landholding patterns, the degree of structural homogeneity in Korean agriculture is striking. Not only is there little variation in the size of holdings, but again cropping patterns do not vary appreciably with the size of operational unit. Most farmers have acquired some paddy land, and their production activities tend to center around rice cultivation with complementary cropping system possibilities dependent on land and labor resources and market accessability. A unimodal structure of small farms means that concerns about relative efficiencies due to differences in operational size are moot, and that research system choices among "efficient" technological improvements are restricted compared to agricultural production systems with large variations in the size of operational holdings (Johnston and Kilby 1975). From both ecological and structural perspectives, agricultural sector homogeneity and heterogeneity are critical factors in agricultural research administration (Berry 1975). Homogeneity simplifies the task in its multiple dimensions—technical, economic, and political.

In light of the previous argument about Korean agricultural sector homogeneity, the Korean research-commodity congruity index figures presented in Table 5-1 do not look particularly robust in comparative, cross-national perspective. The fact that the index declined in the 1970s, while national development, as measured in aggregage economic terms (GNP per capita), continued at a rapid pace suggests that market forces alone were not driving the research resource allocation process. A closer look at what has happened is provided using the author's calculation of research-commodity congruity indices based on internal budget data supplied by ORD.[1] Agricultural research expenditures were disaggregated into four commodity groups: rice, field crops (barley, wheat, soybeans, maize, sweet potatoes, etc.), horticultural crops (vegetables, fruit, Irish potatoes), and livestock. The production value of these commodity groups was taken from official Ministry of Agriculture and Fisheries (MAF) statistical series. Table 5-2 below lists the research-commodity congruity indices calculated from the above data sources for five-year intervals from 1970-1984. Table 5-3 lists the breakdown of commodity group research expenditures and commodity production values (in percentages).

TABLE 5-2. Korean Research-Commodity Congruity Index

Time Periods	Index Value
1970-74	.969
1975-79	.960
1980-84	.975

Sources: Office of Rural Development internal budget data; Ministry of Agriculture and Fisheries (various years).

TABLE 5-3. Research Commodity Percentage Breakdowns

	1970-74		1975-79		1980-84	
Commodity	VA	RE	VA	RE	VA	RE
Rice	46	38	43	33	39	37
Field crops	21	17	15	26	11	24
Horticulture	17	14	24	14	23	14
Livestock	16	31	17	26	27	26

VA = Percentage of value of total agricultural production.
RE = Percentage of total value of research expenditures.

Source: Office of Rural Development internal budget data; Ministry of Agriculture and Fisheries (various years).

The research-commodity congruity indices (Table 5-2), when viewed in isolation, suggest movement toward a more efficient, responsive agricultural research system. However, analysis of the breakdowns of research expenditures over the fifteen-year period (Table 5-3) reveals an increase in the percentage of total research expenditures allocated to staple food crops (rice plus field crops), a decrease in the percentage allocated to livestock research, and a constant percentage spent on research on horticultural crops. These trends run counter to changes in the relative economic importance of these commodity groups over time, as measured by their percentage weights in total value of agricultural production. These trends must also be interpreted in light of data suggesting that livestock and vegetable crops require more research per unit of commodity value to effect significant productivity increases. Evenson (1978:40, Table 10) discovered a substantial variation in research intensities across commodity groups in his analysis of agricultural research expenditure patterns in the United States—research intensities being defined as research expenditures per unit value of the commodity. His data showed the following research intensity patterns (highest to lowest expenditures per value of product): horticultural crops, livestock, and cereals. More recently, Judd, Boyce, and Evenson (1983) have compiled international research intensity data for the

TABLE 5-4. Research Expenditures as a Percentage of the Value of Production for Selected Commodities (1972-1979)[a]

Commodity	Percent Research Expenditure
Poultry	1.64
Beef	1.36
Coffee	1.18
Vegetables	.73
Wheat	.51
Rice	.25
Maize	.23

[a] Percentages calculated for a sample of 26 countries in Africa, Asia, and Latin America (See Judd, Boyce, and Evenson 1983:69 for list of countries included.)

Source: Judd, Boyce, and Evenson (1986, Table 6, p. 92). Modified version used with permission of the University of Chicago Press.

period 1972-1979 which again show that speciality commodities (livestock, coffee, horticulture) have higher research intensities than staple foodgrains. A sample of commodity research intensity values is provided in Table 5-4.

Undoubtably, the research intensity differentials may be attributed, in part, to the weighted social values placed on different commodities. As stated previously, export crops may receive more sustained research attention both for macroeconomic reasons (the need for foreign exchange), due to internal distributions of political and social power, and/or because of skewed research capabilities left over from the colonial period. It is also quite possible that certain agricultural commodities require more resources for equivalent productivity increases for technical biological and ecological reasons. Capital expenditure requirements for livestock research are considerably greater due to the high cost of experimental subjects, materials, and facilities. Horticultural crops, due to the intensity of cultivation systems and environmental fragility, require heavy expenditures on maintenance (e.g., pest resistance) research, and attention must be directed to maintaining the quality of fresh produce. In addition, the complexity of breeding problems in many horticultural crops may make crop improvement programs more costly than is the case in the cereal crops which, as a general rule, have simpler reproductive systems.

Research intensity trends across commodities in the Korean agricultural research system are presented for the period 1962-1984 in Table 5-5. These trends are moving in opposite directions from expectations derived from the works of Boyce and Evenson (1975) and Judd, Boyce, and Evenson (1983, 1986). In addition, both the research intensity trends (Table 5-5) and the disaggregated commodity expenditure and production value trends (Table 5-3) fit neither recent demand shifts nor revealed supply trends for agricultural commodities in Korea. Table 5-6 presents two indicators of changes in the structure of agricultural commodity demand—income and price elasticities of demand and per capita food consumption patterns. As expected in an economy with rapid per capita income growth, consumer demand for agricultural commodities has shifted from income inelastic staple foodgrains (rice and barley) to income elastic "luxury" commodities (fruit, vegetables, and livestock products).

Table 5-7 shows that farmers have been responsive to these changes in consumer demand. The supply trends are revealed in changes in crop acreage and livestock inventories over the period 1962-1980. Rice acreage has remained constant, the acreage planted to field crops has declined precipitously,

TABLE 5-5. Korean Research Intensities (1962-1984)

Time period	Rice	Field Crops	Horticulture	Livestock
1962-66	.55[a]	.48	1.18	2.71
1967-71	.65	.62	.85	2.50
1970-74	1.04	.98	1.05	2.35
1975-79	.73	1.67	.57	1.53
1980-84	1.17	2.58	.73	1.20

[a]Won research expenditure per 1,000 won of commodity value.

Sources: 1962-71, Burmeister (1985:69); 1970-84, Office of Rural Development internal budget data; Ministry of Agriculture and Fisheries (various years).

TABLE 5-6. Trends in Food Commodity Demand in Korea

Income and Price Elasticities of Demand (1970)

Commodity	Urban Income Elasticity	Urban Price Elasticity	Rural Income Elasticity
Rice	-.1	-.4	.06
Barley	-1.0	-1.0	-.2
Fruit	1.0	-1.0	.8
Vegetables	.4	-.8	.8
Beef	1.7	-.48	1.7
Milk	3.5	-.4	3.5

Source: KASS (1972), Michigan State University (1972).

Per Capita Food Consumption (1979/1970)

Commodity	(%)
Rice	99.4
Barley	37.8
Vegetables	204.5
Fruit	174.0
Meat	219.2
Milk	707.1

Source: Kim and Joo (1982).

land allocated to horticultural crops has shown a threefold increase, and livestock inventories (when weighted by product value) have doubled over this period. The revealed preferences for commodities on the supply side have not been mirrored in agricultural research expenditures. The dynamic commodities, horticultural crops and livestock, have received less attention than warranted if one gives credence to the differential research intensity argument presented here.

Summarizing the funding trends in commodity research, the allocative efficiency model based on market forces does not

TABLE 5-7. Agricultural Production Trends: Crop Acreage and Livestock Inventory (1962-1980)

Year	Rice	Field Crops[a]	Horticulture[b]	Livestock[c]
1980	1,233,038	668,627	458,345	208
1979	1,226,873	814,983	429,458	252
1978	1,222,753	943,639	363,136	226
1977	1,230,040	940,123	381,417	164
1976	1,214,904	1,139,750	358,928	176
1975	1,213,144	1,175,288	358,826	138
1974	1,200,314	1,364,587	343,283	148
1973	1,181,718	1,367,340	319,892	142
1972	1,201,021	1,416,566	307,104	124
1971	1,200,364	1,374,296	312,575	114
1970	1,213,353	1,577,042	314,542	119
1969	1,145,600	1,640,279	275,945	126
1968	1,150,816	1,741,867	238,302	146
1967	1,234,628	1,689,486	218,483	118
1966	1,229,304	1,650,406	191,959	107
1965	1,222,754	1,789,490	185,950	105
1964	1,201,339	1,669,059	161,555	100
1963	1,152,600	1,606,090	138,087	n.a.
1962	1,141,250	1,554,086	158,402	n.a.

n.a. = not available

Acreage Units: 1962-70 = cheong-bo (.99 hectare)
                1971-80 = hectare

[a]Includes barley, wheat, pulses, miscellaneous grains.

[b]Includes fruits and vegetables.

[c]Index computed as weighted sum (percentage of total livestock value added) of heads of cattle and hogs and numbers of chickens.

Source: Ministry of Agriculture and Fisheries (various years).

reflect accurately the rationale behind research resource allocation decisions in Korea in the 1970s. The congruity index calculated by the author implies increased efficiency in that a higher index value reflects closer correspondence between agricultural research expenditures per commodity group and the production value of those commodity groups. However, the value of the index increased due to relative increases in spending on commodity groups which seemingly require less expenditure per product value and which are currently stagnant or declining in terms of consumer demand and producer commitment. During the time period under consideration, the agricultural research resource allocation process did not effectively articulate the changing preferences of producers and consumers.

Korean Agricultural Research System Outputs

A key indicator of agricultural research system activity is the number of technological advances produced over a period of time. The development of new crop varieties is perhaps the most visible product of any agricultural research system. To be sure, less tangible products of importance, often complementary inputs to the visible physical outputs, are also produced and disseminated. Cultural practice recommendations and marketing information are obvious examples. The information about crop varieties, however, is well documented and easy to interpret. Table 5-8 lists the number of officially released crop varieties by commodity (or commodity group) produced by ORD from 1963-1980.

Rice ranks preeminent in this accounting. Several factors are responsible. Throughout the period of study, rice has accounted for approximately 40-50% of the total value of agricultural production. It is grown wherever ecologically possible. Organized rice research in Korea goes back to the establishment of an agricultural demonstration farm at Suweon (the current site of ORD) in 1906. As Hayami and Ruttan (1985:280-294) detail, the Japanese colonial regime put significant agrobureaucratic effort into the improvement of rice production capabilities in Korea. Significant increases occurred in paddy acreage and irrigated acreage. Infrastructural improvements were coupled with the introduction of improved rice varieties and increases in fertilizer input per hectare. During the postindependence era, international linkages continued. The most important relationship in terms of rice production was the establishment of a joint cooperative research agreement between ORD and the International Rice Research Institute (IRRI) in the mid-1960s (Kim 1979). New sources of germplasm, possibilities for more rapid generational increases of

TABLE 5-8. Number of ORD Released Varieties (1963-1980)

Year	Rice	Barley	Wheat	Soy-beans	Field[a]	Fruit	Vege-tables	Special[b]
1963	3	0	0	0	0	0	0	0
1964	1	0	0	0	0	0	0	0
1965	0	0	0	0	0	0	0	0
1966	3	0	0	0	0	0	0	0
1967	0	0	0	0	0	0	0	0
1968	1	2	0	0	0	0	0	0
1969	1	0	0	0	1	0	0	0
1970	2	0	2	0	0	0	0	4
1971	1	0	1	1	0	1	0	0
1972	0	0	0	1	1	0	0	1
1973	1	0	0	0	0	0	0	0
1974	1	1	1	0	0	0	0	0
1975	2	2	2	0	1	0	0	1
1976	4	2	2	0	0	0	0	0
1977	5	1	1	0	2	0	0	1
1978	2	0	0	1	3	1	0	2
1979	0	4	0	2	1	0	1	2
1980	3	1	1	0	0	0	1	2
Total	30	13	10	5	9	2	2	13

[a]Field crops include corn and sweet potatoes.

[b]Special crops include sesame, rape, peanuts, stevia, perilla, flax, ramie, and cotton.

Source: Office of Rural Development (1963-1980).

breeding materials, and novel concepts in breeding for an ideal-type rice plant were obtained from the ORD-IRRI relationship. This linkage, in particular, enhanced the productivity (measured by number of varieties released) of the Korean rice varietal development program in the 1970s.

Wheat and barley also rank high on the varietal production list. Continuous varietal development activity occurred in spite of a precipitous decline in acreage and volume of production of these crops during the 1970s. As with rice, both crops are self-pollinated, and their genetic systems have been intensively mapped out relative to many other cultivated crops. This technical feature, of course, facilitates genetic manipulation and may lead to more varietal production per unit of research investment. And international linkages again were important catalysts of crop improvement efforts in Korea. Several ORD plant breeders were trained in midwestern American universities with strong wheat and barley breeding programs. From the late 1950s to the mid-1970s, bilateral aid agreements between the Korean government and USAID (U.S. Agency for International Development) provided technical agricultural assistance for institution building in agricultural research. U.S. agricultural scientists were sent to Korea under this program. Expatriate scientists who were wheat and barley breeders were instrumental in developing strong Korean breeding programs in these commodities.

It is useful to contrast the wheat and barley situation with that in the horticultural crops. In the latter, we find a robust consumer demand and significant increases in farm acreage, but little research system output in terms of new variety production. Genetically, several of the important Korean "kimchi" vegetables (peppers, chinese cabbage, oriental radishes) are difficult to work with due to cross-pollination and genetic incompatability mechanisms in their reproductive systems. Technically, these crops may require relatively high research intensities. However, there is little evidence to suggest that a systematic attempt has been made within ORD to recruit, train, and support a critical mass of researchers to work on developing breeding programs in the horticultural crops. Complaints were heard, especially within the Horticultural Experiment Station, about the lack of budgetary and personnel support for their endeavors—in contrast to what they felt was an overinvestment in rice research activities within ORD.

Livestock is also a rapidly growing commodity and has become increasingly important for the farm enterprise. It is difficult to quantify the output of the Livestock Experiment Station. Interviews with scientists and administrators suggest that a fairly sustained effort was made to cross-breed Korean native cattle with foreign stock to develop an ecologically adapted animal with higher meat production potential. This program seems to have had relatively little effect at the farm level. Significant numbers of beef and dairy cattle have been imported in recent years to upgrade the quality of the domestic livestock herds. Other research initiatives have centered on forage improvement, pastureland reclamation, and feed ration efficiency. The government has pushed livestock production in the 1980s as a means to increase deteriorating (relative to urban household) farm household incomes. Livestock production, however, remains almost completely dependent on foreign feedgrain imports. Attempts to increase domestic pasture acreage through grassland reclamation projects on steep slopes have foundered on technical problems which make reclamation prohibitively expensive. More recently, "import substitution" efforts have centered on the development of winter forage production on paddy land. It remains to be seen whether some cropping system modifications can integrate crop with livestock production in a way that increases the domestic livestock feed component. The lack of domestic feedgrain and pasture production potential makes domestic beef cattle production an economically problematic venture. More success has accompanied efforts to boost the efficiency of swine and poultry production through increases in the operational size of production units, although again, these enterprises are dependent on imported feedstuffs.

The other indicator of research output frequently used in measurements of agricultural research system performance is the number of research publications. Boyce and Evenson (1975), Evenson and Kislev (1975), and Judd, Boyce, and Evenson (1983) have used publication counts as proxies for the creation of knowledge and measures of relative commodity emphasis in their cross-national studies of investment in agricultural research. Questions inevitably arise about the validity of publication counts as indicators of scientific productivity. Scientists' publication motives are multifaceted (Busch and Lacy 1983). Publications often reflect the scientist's drive for professional status. Research that generates publications may be tailored as much by the availability of equipment and convenience as by systematic attention to unresolved problems of scientific import. Scientific publications are often claimed to have little technical and/or economic utility in the everyday world of crop production. Evenson and others would argue, however, that seemingly esoteric research is often translated into practical knowledge, and, as a result, publications are an important measure of research system activities and priorities.

Table 5-9 shows the stock of research publications by commodity groups for Korea during the 1970s. Judd, Boyce, and Evenson (1983:68-69, Appendix Table 3) have published an inventory of research publications by country using the *Commonwealth Agricultural Bureau Abstracts (CABA)*. This abstract series is one of the most complete sources of agricultural research publication outputs. Their data for the periods 1972-1975 and 1976-1979 reveal commodity emphases similar to those found in the analyses of budget expenditures.

TABLE 5-9. Number of Korean Research Publications by Commodity Group (1963-1979)

ORD Research Publications

Commodity Group	1963-66	1967-70	1971-74	1975-78
Rice	38 (28)	61 (27)	63 (30)	62 (27)
Field crops[a]	20 (15)	35 (15)	29 (14)	50 (22)
Horticulture[b]	19 (14)	43 (19)	37 (17)	32 (14)
Livestock	57 (43)	91 (40)	83 (39)	88 (38)

Note: Figures in parentheses are commodity percentages of total research publication output for specified years.

[a]Field crops include barley, wheat, maize, soybeans, field beans, and sweet potatoes.

[b]Horticultural crops include vegetables, fruit, and Irish potatoes.

Source: Office of Rural Development (1963-1979).

Commonwealth Agricultural Bureau Abstracts

Commodity Group	1972-75	1976-79
Rice	177 (57)	166 (39)
Field crops	52 (17)	81 (19)
Vegetables	26 (8)	37 (9)
Livestock	56 (18)	141 (33)

Source: Judd, Boyce, and Evenson (1983:68-69).

Horticultural crops are decidedly underrepresented, accounting for less than 10% of total research publications in either time period. Rice and field crops combined remain relatively prominent in the stock of publications, accounting for over 50% of the total in either time period. An upswing in livestock research publications is noted, a trend that parallels the growing importance of the livestock industry in Korea. For comparative purposes, the author tabulated by commodity group the official research publications released by ORD for the period 1963-1978. The low level of horticultural publications mirrored *CABA* data. Livestock publications as a percentage of total published research reports were somewhat higher for ORD than for *CABA* tabulations, although unlike the *CABA* data, there was no significant gain in the relative percentage of published livestock research. Given the range of commodities in the horticultural and livestock sectors and the biological and ecological complexity of advances in productivity in these commodities, the publication data presented here reinforce conclusions drawn from the analysis of budget data. These two commodity sectors have not received research attention commensurate with their increasing importance in Korean agriculture.

The Visible Hand of the State in Agricultural Research Resource Allocation

The percentage shift in research spending toward rice and field crops, at the expense of livestock and horticultural crops, tells the story of the relative import of state power and market power in agricultural research policymaking during the 1970s. Basically, the government's push for rice self-sufficiency outlined in the last chapter has skewed research resource allocation within the system. From 1970-1974 to 1980-1984 the combined percentage of the agricultural research budget allocated to rice and field crops increased from 55% to 61%, while the total production value of these commodity groups decreased from 67% to 50%. The reasons for this emphasis on food staples was outlined in the last chapter—macroeconomic concern about increased grain imports was the paramount catalyst of foodgrain self-sufficiency policies.

Attempts to encourage self-sufficiency in foodgrains through measures to increase supply (including agricultural research) were complemented by changes in price policies and rationing measures designed to encourage the substitution of barley for rice. Consumer prices for barley were readjusted downward relative to rice prices in order to induce foodgrain substitution. If this were not enough, the government mandated "rice-less" days for restaurants and public institutions, forbade the use of rice in the brewing of traditional Korean liquors, decreed the use of smaller rice bowls in restaurants to cut down on food waste, and stipulated the serving of a fixed rice/barley mixture in restaurants and other institutional settings. All of these measures were designed to alter the per capita consumption of foodgrains in a way that decreased rice import requirements.

The historical and social context of rice and coarse grain consumption explains the difficulty in achieving this goal, in spite of the government's use of an array of pricing and rationing policy instruments. Barley and other coarse grains have always been considered inferior foods in the Korean diet. Rice was the preferred staple; barley and other substitutes were eaten by poor people and during periods of "summer famine" when rice supplies ran low prior to the fall harvest. The Japanese colonial legacy reinforced these consumption attitudes, as the Japanese confiscated Korean rice to supply the home islands and the Koreans were forced to substitute coarse grains imported from Manchuria in line with compulsory trade flows within the integrated Greater East Asian Co-Prosperity Sphere. During the 1970s, a variant of this "grain arbitrage" strategy was revived by the Korean government in their effort to achieve foodgrain self-sufficiency. This goal was to be achieved by simultaneously increasing rice production and encouraging more substitution of domestically produced barley for rice. However, the rising incomes of the average Korean consumer meant that inferior staples were increasingly less likely to be substituted for rice, regardless of government-dictated price differentials. As shown in Table 5-7, government policies promoting barley consumption did not halt the precipitous decline in barley acreage. As rice consumption leveled off (Table 5-6) and domestic supplies have increased, the government gradually relaxed measures to induce or compel barley/rice substitution. Barley price supports for producers and controls on the consumption of rice were gradually being withdrawn in the early 1980s.

The other important staple cereal in the Korean diet is wheat. Wheat was not a traditional food in Korea. It has become an important commodity in the postindependence era due to its concessionary availability under the U.S. PL 480 program during the 1950s and 1960s. Dietary patterns were altered, as Koreans became acclimated to eating a variety of wheat products. The U.S. withdrawal of concessionary wheat supplies in the 1970s, as mentioned in Chapter 4, meant that wheat imports might eventually require substantial hard currency outflows. There was administrative support within the agrobureaucracy for a crash wheat breeding and production program to alleviate some of the projected foreign exchange drain. The world commodity market situation in the early 1970s provided further impetus to import substitution leanings, as it appeared that scarce quantities and high prices might make reliance on external supplies of essential foodstuffs a high risk gamble. Earlier technical studies in Korea projected substantial latitude for expansion of domestic wheat acreage, particularly the substitution of wheat for less preferred barley as the winter crop in paddy double-crop rotations. Unfortunately, optimism about wheat production possibilities proved to be largely unfounded (Desrosiers, Kopf, and Yohe 1978). High humidity and temperature fluctuations in the spring affected wheat more adversely than the traditional barley varieties that improved wheat cultivars were supposed to replace. And, as mentioned in Chapter 4, the newly developed Tongil rice varieties required accompanying double-cropped wheat or barley complements with early fall planting and early spring ripening potential, further compounding the technical problems of cropping system synchronization.

The establishment of a separate Wheat and Barley Research Institute within ORD in 1977 provides insight into how research initiatives emerge in the Korean setting. The Minister of Agriculture at that time was concerned about increasing wheat imports, in line with concerns throughout the bureaucracy about the impending leakage of scarce foreign exchange for agricultural products. He asked wheat breeders in ORD if it was technically feasible to cut imports by 50%, producing approximately 600,000 metric tons of wheat domestically. The scientists replied that they had good breeding stocks, and with sustained financial commitment, they could develop in five years improved winter wheat cultivars that could successfully replace declining barley in paddy double-crop systems. The bureaucratic response to this prospect was the formation of a separate institute for wheat research. Although the rationale paralleled that of the Tongil campaign, interest in the project was not sustained within the bureaucracy, and the initiative failed to achieve any measureable results. In fact, wheat has almost disappeared from the Korean crop portfolio. Domestic wheat prices are no longer supported above world price levels, and domestically produced wheat now accounts for a miniscule 2% of domestic consumption. As wheat cultivation has almost disappeared, the wheat research emphasis has given way to a focus on barley in the Wheat and Barley Research Institute. Increasing labor bottlenecks in the countryside have made double cropping of winter cereals a more problematic enterprise, from both operational and economic standpoints. Increasing labor costs and declining price supports have rendered traditional labor intensive double-cropping practices unprofitable. The government is now promoting more mechanization as the solution, but the development of cost-efficient small farm tractors with interchangeable implements for flooded rice and dry field winter cereal cultivation and harvesting is complex. Given the cropping systems implications of winter cereals cultivation, the spin-off of a separate institute for winter cereals seems counterproductive. Physical separation of research facilities—previously both rice and winter cereals research were conducted at the Crop Experiment Station—has made it difficult for scientists to collaborate on the cropping systems implications of their work, leaving scientists at the Wheat and Barley Research Institute to work on rather esoteric problems, such as breeding for grain characteristics that make barley similar in physical appearance and cooking qualities to the preferred staple, rice.

Another example of this centralized mode of research priority setting and resource allocation is the "Olympic vegetable initiative." After Korea was awarded the Olympic games in 1981, concern began to be voiced in the highest government policymaking circles about how best to accommodate foreign visitors. The Olympics have been billed by the present ruling group as Korea's rite of passage to advanced industrial status within the world community, and every effort is to being made to insure the success of the event. One point of discussion centered around the need to provide western-type foods for foreign guests. The spicy Korean cuisine, after all, might be too potent for the uninitiated. The Horticultural Experiment Station was then directed to start work on the production of vegetables agreeable to western palates, such as potatoes suitable for french-frying. This initiative became somewhat of a joke within research circles, although the humor was tempered by a certain amount of resentment over the fact that research resources were being allocated on a priority basis to accommodate pampered foreigners, rather than being directed to the real needs of Korean producers and consumers. The centralized administrative and budgetary system makes it possible to direct resources quickly to special projects as outlined above, but often with little effective feedback from either researchers or the end-users of research.

This lack of clientele responsiveness is especially apparent in the miniscule portion of the agricultural research budget allocated to marketing and other farm management problems. Calculations based on internal budget data supplied to the author by ORD show that for the period 1979-1984, on the average, 1.6% of the total annual research budget was allocated for farm management research. This is an especially revealing statistic in light of the increasing market orientation of Korean agriculture. During the last decade, there has been a decided shift away from subsistence-oriented staple foodgrain production to the production of a wide variety of vegetable and fruit crops for the market. Agricultural production "guidance" from above—exhortations and advice from extension agents and other local government officials—relating to rice production targets during the Tongil campaign was overbearing, while farmers were left to fend for themselves in the more complex world of fruit and vegetable production and marketing. Wade (1983:15) notes that the ratio of extension agents to farm households and cultivated area (one officer/240 farm households and 200 hectares) ranks the Korean agrobureaucracy among the most dense, penetrating rural government structures in the developing world. Farmers complain that they see extension agents as many as three times a day during the peak rice growing season, as they are constantly monitored and receive a barrage of instructions pertaining to pest control and fertilization passed down from MAF/ORD channels. Extension agents are perceived by many farmers to be trained only in rice production techniques, unable to provide the needed technical backup support in other commodity areas. Farmers rely on their peers for cultivation and marketing information about other commodities. At the farm level, state, rather than societal, priorities are articulated in the everyday communication and advice relayed through formal agricultural research and extension channels.

Notes

1. A brief note on the sources for the Korean agricultural research expenditure data utilized in Tables 5-2, 5-3, and 5-5 is warranted. Published government budget data do not disaggregate ORD agricultural research expenditures into commodity-specific accounting categories. The author received hand-written ORD budget breakdowns for each central ORD research institute from ORD officials for the years 1962-1984. Research expenditures for commodity groups were calculated from this data base. Explanations of procedures for calculating commodity group research expenditures are presented in Burmeister (1985, Appendix C). The commodity group research expenditure data presented in tabular form in the above reference were updated for research-commodity congruity index calculations in this monograph. The complete research expenditure series used may be obtained from the author upon request. Similar time series data on Korean agricultural research and extension budgets is found in Park (1986, Appendix C.

6
Scientist Decision Making Within the Office of Rural Development: Authority and Influence Patterns

Recent work in organization theory emphasizes the adaptation of organizations to the wider social, economic, and political environments in which they are embedded (Aldrich 1979). The Korean state/society relationship was analyzed in Chapter 3. The Office of Rural Development (ORD), the government agricultural research and extension organization, was reorganized in 1962 shortly after General Park's ascent to power. The sociopolitical context in which resources for agricultural research and extension were made available influenced types of relationships both within the research organization and between the organization and significant external actors. In keeping with the overriding theme of this monograph, the relative impact of state and societal pressures on agricultural research decision making has been assessed by asking ORD scientists about their work environment, work activities, and communication patterns.

Insights drawn from two substantive specialties within sociology, organization theory and the sociology of science, provide important investigative leads. A synthesis of these perspectives is required to explain the dynamics of scientific activity in the world of "corporate or Baconian" science (Busch and Lacy 1983)—that is, large scientific research organizations. When policymakers began to recognize that national scientific development was a precondition for economic growth and military capability—a trend that was well under way by the latter half of the nineteenth century—investment in scientific infrastructure became another necessary state intervention to secure a competitive position for particular nation-states in the world political economy.

The problem of large-scale, bureaucratically administered scientific programs is interesting because of the perceived antinomies of routinized bureaucratic efficiency and the relatively unstructured environment necessary for scientific creativity. Scientists in industry, for example, have been studied in an attempt to assess the compatability of bureaucratic authority structures with the patterns of open communication, work flexibility, and collegial interpersonal relations deemed necessary for scientific advance (Kornhauser 1962; Pelz and Andrews 1976). While the avowed objective of corporate scientific effort has been to establish a facilitative environment for the working scientist, there is apprehension that the end result may be stifling bureaucratic regimentation.

A closed polity is often thought to make this intrinsic problem of bureaucratic science even more intractable (Merton 1973:254-266). When an administrative culture discourages accountability to a wider public, extraorganizational linkages to civilian groups are minimized. When state policies restrict the growth of organizations representing societal interests or ideological barriers are raised to the pursuit of inquiry, communication channels and the resulting flow of information are constricted. In the language of Aldrich's (1979) population ecology model, the number of interorganizational linkages may be drastically reduced and organizational dependence on a narrow support base encouraged, thus limiting the responsiveness of the research organization to a wider range of stimuli. This problem seems especially acute in "consumer-oriented" applied scientific efforts where success is judged in part by user adoption and satisfaction. Agricultural technology is a case in point. Farmers willingly adopt new technologies on the basis of perceived gains. If exclusionary statism accurately describes the Korean state/society relationship in the 1970s and early 1980s, these issues are clearly outstanding in analyzing intra- and interorganizational relationships in the Korean agricultural research system.

Research Decisions: Whose Preferences Count?

Sociological explanations of scientific research activities explore both internal and external social influences. Merton's (1973) pioneering work on the value system of science stressed the "internal" dimension. This emphasis on the normative structure of science and the tendency to conceptualize science as an autonomous subsystem of society have lost favor with the gradual demise of functionalism as the hegemonic paradigm in American sociology (Mulkay 1979). Yet studies of the scientific community that emphasize its unique occupational or professional status remain exemplars in the sociology of science genre. The distinctive patterns of social interaction and social stratification that separate the world of science from other social worlds have become focal points for explanations of scientific behavior and research decision making (Hagstrom 1965; Cole and Cole 1973; Crane 1972).

Busch and Lacy (1983) explored "internalist" influences on scientific activity in their pathbreaking study of the agricultural science community in the United States. These authors examined the social and educational backgrounds of scientists, communication patterns that sustain scientific inquiry, and the impact of disciplinary identification on attitudes and work patterns. Not surprisingly, scientists accorded priority in their work lives to problem agendas constructed within disciplinary worlds. Career advancement and professional recognition were often fashioned in this arena.

Busch and Lacy noted the crucial link between the production of scientific publications and career advancement in the United States. Publications must pass through "gatekeepers" (journal editors and peer reviewers) who stress standardized scientific research procedures, experimental designs that maximize statistical robustness, and philosophical strictures about "legitimate" and "cumulative" contributions to the extant stock of scientific knowledge. These requirements, in a sense, delimit research possibilities for the upwardly mobile scientist. The demand for statistical robustness, for example, may require degrees of experimental control that shape the objectives and objects of inquiry. Randomization and replication, the golden rules of experimental design, favor research projects based on short duration experiments in tightly controlled environments. Such "internal" scientific influences may be important determinants of research decision making and activity.

Sociologists who have analyzed the unique internal social structure of science do not deny that extrascientific social pressures also influence scientific activities. Very early in his scholarly career, Merton (1973:191-210) recognized the economic and military demands for advanced technology in the capital accumulation and state building processes that characterize modern world system dynamics. For some sociologists, science has become such a vital cog in the world political economy that scientists have assumed a strategic position within the social division of labor. Bell (1973) and Gouldner (1979), from quite different theoretical perspectives, have elevated scientists to the position of the new social elite in "advanced industrial" or "postcapitalist" society.

The relationship between "internal" and "external" determinants of scientific activity is interactive. External pressures are selectively filtered through the internal social structure of science in accommodating ways. In the western capitalist democracies, for example, "external" social demands for scientific research are recognized in the course of the political budgeting process. At the same time, scientific activity is allowed to proceed relatively unencumbered within the particular social context that defines the "internal" scientific world.

This outcome has been described in analytical terms for the agricultural sciences by agricultural economists. As stated in Chapter 5, the measurement of the economic returns to agricultural research show that research investments have been quite productive. An institutional affinity is posited between the social structure of science and the structure of the market in advanced capitalist societies. This argument is found in the induced innovation literature (Hayami and Ruttan 1971:56-59; Ruttan 1975:188-191; Evenson and Binswanger 1978:164-184; Ruttan 1982, Chs. 2-3). An analogy between the supply-demand forces in neoclassical economics is used to describe how "internal" and "external" pressures for scientific output come together in a socially productive manner. The rigors of competition in both the economic market and the world of the professional scientist (the unceasing quest for peer recognition for priority in scientific discovery or competition in the marketplace of ideas) provide a facilitative social environment for efficient (Pareto optimal) technological change.

Furthermore, in the course of economic development, a differentiated demand-supply responsiveness has been achieved within the scientific community as evidenced by the complementary division of labor between basic research and adaptive research that characterizes the output of a balanced agricultural research program. This complementary division of labor depends upon organizational structures and/or political linkages that facilitate communications between research administrators, scientists, extension agents, and their clientele.

Induced innovation proponents often point to the land grant research-education-extension complex in the United States as an exemplar of organizational synergy (the university linked to the experiment station) and political accountability (decentralized funding through state legislatures). Facilitative intra- and interorganizational relationships have emerged to ensure effective articulation of demand and supply for publicly funded agricultural research (Evenson, Waggoner, and Ruttan 1979).

In the above scenario, both organized clientele groups able to exert effective political influence and a strong, independent cadre of scientists are necessary for effective public sector agricultural research initiatives. Scientists must be accountable to other social groups if their work is to be financed from the public treasury. But scientists must also have a degree of freedom to pursue research topics which may appear esoteric to the uninitiated. Basic science breakthroughs are inherently unpredictable and, to a degree, serendipitous.

The existence of organized interest groups does not guarantee that effective influence is socially neutral. The farmers with the best asset portfolios are likely to reap the largest benefits from technological "reinvigoration" of the factors of production. It is also likely that they will become the most articulate and effective political supporters of public sector agricultural research. In capitalist societies, the social welfare ambiguity of effective demand for research is further compounded by the commodity-based priorities of research. As Busch and Lacy's (1983) study points out, social resources which are not commodified—community and the ecosystem to name two of the most important—may be neglected in publicly funded agricultural research programs.

The brief discussion of the development of the agricultural research and extension complex in the United States in Chapter 2 reminds us that clientele groups may be in part administrative creations of the state. Because of the state's sponsorship of agricultural research activity, administrative authority needs to be considered alongside scientific and clientele influences as a dominant social force in the establishment of agricultural research priorities. As we have repeated on several occasions, the state is no mere cipher through which private interests are filtered. State officials may articulate and promulgate programs in support of self-aggrandizement and/or national advancement aims. State officials' interest in fostering viable scientific research programs is a logical outcome of the correlation between technological advance, economic growth, military capability, upward ascent in the interstate system, and their own political longevity. State supported science has become a taken-for-granted policy instrument in efforts to achieve and/or sustain competitive viability in the world political economy.

In this chapter, the unit of analysis is the individual researcher within Korea's Office of Rural Development. The basic question at hand is the relative power of significant actors—administrators, other scientists, interest groups—to influence what ORD scientists do. Organization theorists Bacharach and Lawler (1980:44) make a useful distinction between authority and influence as contrasting types of power relationships within the formal organization. Authority relationships are structural, formal, centralized patterns of obligations and communications that bind together a hierarchy of ranked officeholders in the organization; influence relationships are informal, often voluntary, multidirectional relationships that bring people with similar interests or characteristics together in everyday organizational life. In the context of this study, authority signifies state power; influence represents societal power (scientific influence and clientele influence). Within the domain of the formal organization, authority and influence are always present. At issue here is the balance of these power relationships as this balance conditions the everyday work lives of agricultural researchers working in a "corporate" scientific organization, the Office of Rural Development. The balance should, in turn, be related to the type of state/society relationship within which the organization is embedded.

If the exclusionary statist appellation fits the Korean state/society relationship during the period under consideration, one may ask whether "soft admiminstration" in agricultural research can coexist with a "hard state." A "softly" administered agricultural research system is one that is accountable to clients and provides freedom of inquiry and an effective participatory voice for researchers. The conventional wisdom about the location specificity of agricultural research requires that both attributes of softness be present to some degree if suitable technologies are to be developed. The "hard state," by contrast, is able to place obligations on lower-level government officials to promulgate economic development initiatives mandated by the highest-ranking state policymakers. This ability resides in a bureaucratic structure where discretionary controls and mechanisms of compulsion make it difficult for government employees to evade or refashion policies handed down from above (see Jones and Sakong 1980:132-140). Even scientists, a group with considerable social autonomy by virtue of possession of specialized knowledge, are not immune from hierarchical control strictures. In fact, the literature on the bureaucratic-authoritarian mode of social domination in third world societies stresses how scientific expertise may be enlisted by state officials as an "efficient technocratic" substitute for societal bargaining in public policy formulation and implementation.

Power relationships find concrete expression in work activities, communication patterns, and work attitudes. A survey instrument administered to a random stratified sample of ORD scientists was designed to obtain information on the above behavioral and attitudinal patterns. Indicators of administrative authority, scientific influence, and clientele influence were constructed as measures of power relationships operative within ORD. Face validity is the predominant logical rationale for the indicators developed. Included in the questionnaire were Likert-type attitude questions, ranking exercises, and factual questions about the work situation. The design of the research instrument was influenced by the previous work of Busch, Lacy, and Sachs (1980). The complete questionnaire form, details of its administration, a discussion of the limitation of this type of information collecting device, and information about ancillary open-ended interviews with research administrators are provided in Appendix 6-A at the end of this chapter.

ORD Organizational Structure

Before proceeding with the substantive analysis of how different types of social power relationships influence everyday scientific activities within ORD, a brief sketch of ORD organizational structure is necessary. As was noted in Chapter 5, there are distinct divisions of labor within the central institutes of ORD. These central institutes (CORDs) are organized either around commodities (Crop Experiment Station, Horticultural Experiment Station, Wheat and Barley Research Institute, Livestock Experiment Station, etc.), regions (Yeongnam and Honam Crop Experiment Stations, Alpine Experiment Station, Cheju Experiment Station), factors of production (Agricultural Mechanization Institute), or basic science endeavors

(Institute of Agricultural Sciences). Scientists in the crop production-related CORD institutes are charged with developing new crop varieties, investigating problems in crop physiology and soil fertility, and examining new cultural practices and crop production strategies. Comparable research agendas have been adopted in the livestock-related institutes. Within the Korean context, this work represents the basic science continuum of agricultural research efforts.

There are also provincial ORD (PORD) research stations located in each province that are attached to the provincial government administrative apparatus. The PORDs are responsible for adaptation research. New technologies generated by the CORDs are passed down to PORDs for location-specific testing, modification, and/or cultural practice recommendations. The PORDs comprise, in effect, the applied research arm of ORD. South Korea is a small country. The fact that there are nine provincial research stations, along with four other CORD regional branch experiment stations, suggests that the ORD system is a decentralized one. This characteristic is accorded much importance in the literature on agricultural research policy (Ruttan 1982). The reason for the emphasis on decentralization is, of course, because applications of agricultural research are often quite location specific, in contrast to applications of industrial research which can often be diffused widely with minimal disruption of production results. Thus, conventional wisdom holds that to be effective, agricultural research systems must be decentralized.

However, in the literature, the decentralization of agricultural research activities has taken on a broader connotation. Decentralization also connotes elements of local political control. The land-grant complex in the United States is politically decentralized in that state government units appropriate public monies for research programs. Theoretically, through this appropriations process, societal interests may exert appreciable influence on the direction of agricultural research policy. Thus, a "political economy" consequence of decentralization is the effective political linkage between the agricultural research enterprise and an end-user clientele. The ORD system is not decentralized in a political sense. As was mentioned briefly in Chapter 3, the Ministry of Home Affairs is responsible for all local government functions at provincial and lower unit levels. All officials are appointed by the central ministry; local government funding consists mainly of grants to local government from national government coffers. The Park regime deliberately consolidated all legislative and budgetary authority at the national level. The Korean governmental apparatus, including the ORD arm, is best described as a "deconcentrated" rather than a decentralized system (Jacobs 1985). Functional units of government were organized in the provinces and its county and township subdivisions, but this deconcentration was designed to effect control rather than to encourage representation and accountability.

CORD and PORD respondents have been separated in this analysis for two reasons. First, the aforementioned division of labor distinguishes each subgroup. Because the CORDs have more basic research responsibilities in the Korean agricultural scientific context, this group of scientists is expected to be more responsive to scientific influences. Second, CORD and PORD scientists differ in social background characteristics. Educational backgrounds should predispose CORD scientists to be more attuned to the demands of the scientific reward system, as approximately 55% of the CORD respondents in the sample had advanced educational degrees, compared to 30% of the PORD research scientists. PORD workers, on the other hand, should be more responsive to administrative pressures given the direct link of PORD operations to provincial government development bureaucracies and the applied nature of PORD responsibilities. PORD scientists would also seem more likely to be influenced by clientele pressures than their CORD cohorts. Over 90% of the PORD scientists in the sample worked in their home province, compared with only 15% of the CORD sample, and a larger percentage of PORD researchers came from rural backgrounds (71% compared to 55% of the CORD scientists). PORD scientists appear to be socially and physically more proximate to the end-users of the research product. These social background characteristics are posited as possible intervening variables conditioning the relative impact of administrative, scientific, and clientele pressures in the research decision-making process of CORD and PORD scientists.

Administrative Authority and ORD Scientist Behavior

If state power is a driving force in establishing the research agenda in Korea, expectations are that administrative authority relations will be prominent in influencing decision making and determining the activities of ORD scientists. Ideally, organizational relationships in scientific bureaucracies are designed to foster coordination among workers and facilitate access to other resources. Thus, the superior-subordinate ties may be more collegial than traditional chain-of-command organizational stereotypes imply. But if the research organization is in part a mobilization agency, goals, methods, and timetables sent down from higher levels may take precedence over scientist-initiated activity based on scientific and/or clientele feedback.

Several categories of information were included in the survey questionnaire to examine the orientation of Korean agricultural scientists toward administrative authority. Examples include the amount of time spent by scientists in administrative work, the perceived importance of organizational goals on research decision making, the perceived ability to coordinate research activities across disciplines and institutes, and the perceived freedom of inquiry within the organization. Indicators of administrative authority are presented in Table 6-1. For each indicator cited in the following tables, the coded indicator name, the question and response categories on which the indicator is based, and the responses of both CORD and PORD scientists are given (recorded as percentages).

While both CORD and PORD scientists believed that they had flexibility in determining their own research agendas (FRESULT and FTOPIC), responses to other indicators suggest that administrative pressures were strong.[1] Data collated on the indicators ORDGOAL, BOSS, and SCIADMR suggested a top-down approach to research decision making. Both CORD and PORD scientists (91% CORD, 88% PORD) cited "direct relationship to ORD goals for agricultural development" (ORDGOAL) as either a "very important" or "somewhat important" reason for undertaking current or recently completed research projects. Similarly, "assignment by my superior" (BOSS) was ranked a "very important" or "somewhat important" reason for working on research projects by 69% of CORD and 63% of PORD scientist respondents. The SCIADMR indicator is especially significant, as 53% of CORD and 62% of PORD scientists disagreed or strongly disagreed with the following statement: "The relationship between scientists and administrators at our institute is more collegial than supervisory." In the world of corporate science, the scientist-administrator must be able to cushion political (administrative) demands in ways that maximize decision-making latitude for the working

TABLE 6-1. Administrative Authority Indicators (percent)

FRESULT (1) I have much freedom to interpret research results.

	CORD	PORD
Strongly agree	19	21
Agree	55	36
Uncertain	15	24
Disagree	9	17
Strongly disagree	3	0

FTOPIC (7) I have a reasonable amount of freedom to choose my own research topics.

	CORD	PORD
Strongly agree	8	38
Agree	48	43
Uncertain	29	12
Disagree	13	7
Strongly disagree	1	0

Rank the importance of each of the following reasons for working on particular research projects:

ORDGOAL (20j) Direct relationship to ORD goals for agricultural development.

	CORD	PORD
Very important	40	51
Somewhat important	51	37
Of little importance	8	7
Least important	1	2

BOSS (20d) Assignment by my superior.

	CORD	PORD
Very important	10	22
Somewhat important	59	41
Of little importance	24	29
Least important	7	7

TABLE 6-1. Continued

SCIADMR (5)	The relationship between scientists and administrators at our institute is more collegial than supervisory.

	CORD	PORD
Strongly agree	0	5
Agree	23	19
Uncertain	24	14
Disagree	36	48
Strongly disagree	17	14

TADM (16c)	Amount of work time spent on administrative activities (filling out official forms and writing official reports).

	CORD	PORD
0-10%	21	15
11-20%	28	32
21-30%	20	37
31+%	32	17

ADMPRESS (19d)	Rank the importance of "bad research atmosphere due to administrative pressures" to ORD performance.

	CORD	PORD
Very important	49	70
Somewhat important	48	22
Least important	3	8

COOPPART (2)	If I spend time working outside my institute on cooperative projects, it will be difficult for me to complete my work assignments.

	CORD	PORD
Strongly agree	20	26
Agree	40	33
Uncertain	11	21
Disagree	24	17
Strongly disagree	5	2

TABLE 6-1. Continued

MULDISOP (11)   If a scientist wants to advance in ORD, it is better to focus one's attention on work within the institute rather than to participate in multidisciplinary research with other institutes.

	CORD	PORD
Strongly agree	12	2
Agree	27	40
Uncertain	27	17
Disagree	28	31
Strongly disagree	7	10

Numbers in parentheses refer to the item number in the original questionnaire (see Appendix 6-A).

Percentage totals may not add to 100 due to rounding errors.

scientists. The role of scientist-administrator is that of mediator between the worlds of politics and science. In ORD, however, working scientists often defined the administrator's hierarchical position in the organization rather than her/his scientific status as the predominant social definition of the on-the-job relationship, suggesting that balance between the worlds of politics and science is difficult to achieve in this organizational setting.

The weight of administrative authority within the research organization was revealed further in responses about how scientists spent time on the job. Over half of both CORD and PORD scientists reported spending over 20% of their work time on routine administrative tasks such as filling out official forms and writing official reports (TADM). These scientist respondents, it must be remembered, had no formal administrative or supervisory responsibilities (see Appendix 6-A for sample characteristics). Furthermore, 49% of CORD scientists and 70% of PORD scientists ranked administrative pressures as very important (in a negative sense) to ORD performance (ADMPRESS).

The ability to engage in scientific work which spanned institute boundaries is tapped in the indicators MULDISOP and COOPPART. A plurality of both CORD (39%) and PORD (42%) respondents either agreed or strongly agreed with the statement that it is better to focus one's attention on work within the institute, rather than participate in multidisciplinary work across institutes, if one wants to advance in ORD (MULDISOP). A majority of both CORD (60%) and PORD (59%) respondents either agreed or strongly agreed with the statement that it was difficult to complete work assignments if one participated in cooperative research projects with other institutes (COOPPART). This reticence about collaborative work between institutes suggests a hierarchical management control structure that confines research activities within particular institutes.

In summary, administrative pressures appeared as significant determinants of research decision making in the work lives of both CORD and PORD scientists. PORD scientists, as expected, showed somewhat more sensitivity to direct administrative interference on a few indicators (e.g., a higher percentage of PORD respondents chose the strongest response categories for the items ADMPRESS, BOSS, and ORDGOAL). It appears, however, that administrative authority strongly permeates the entire ORD structure, even though CORD and PORD institutes have somewhat different research responsibilities and are located in distinctly different positions vis-à-vis other state bureaucratic agencies.

Clientele Influence and ORD Scientist Behavior

The literature on agricultural research systems stresses the need for farmer-researcher communication if appropriate technological innovations are to be developed. Direct farmer access to the research organization may occur through organized interest group lobbying, agricultural research review boards incorporating the targeted farmer clientele, legislative bodies responsible for budgeting and program review, and/or official organizational channels of communication which bring the agrobureaucracy in direct contact with farmers. Indirect farmer access to researchers has been routinized through extension agent intermediaries, agricultural specialists whose job it is to inform researchers at the experiment station about current and anticipated production problems at the farm level. This information is the product of recurrent consultations between extension agents and farmers. Indirect clientele influence on the agricultural research process may also occur as a result of other socialization experiences. Formal training in the agricultural science disciplines within specialized colleges of agriculture may contain a deliberate inculcation of a service "mission." Or, in a more informal fashion, receptivity to farmers and farm problems may result from the farm family backgrounds of agricultural scientists.

At the onset of the 1980s, the first three direct means of clientele (farmer) access to working scientists were quite restricted in Korea. Formal meetings bringing ORD scientists and farmers together occurred during the winter months, mainly as training sessions to diffuse new technologies. Indirect means of farmer-researcher communication were institutionalized via the extension service (Rural Guidance Office is the best English translation for this ORD bureau). Official government explanations of ORD organizational structure stress that communication between key agricultural sector actors was facilitated by the administrative placement of the research and extension (R & E) bureaus under the unified ORD umbrella. This organizational structure supposedly avoided the bifurcation of objectives and activities often attributed to the bureaucratic separation of research and extension. In light of the paucity of voluntary associations at the regional and local levels, effective operation of these institutionalized bureaucratic communication channels became essential for adequate information flows between the farm and the research station.

The logic of operationalization for clientele influence indicators is simple. Measures were sought that registered the amount of direct contact between researchers and extension agents and between researchers and farmers. In addition, researchers were asked to respond to attitudinal questions about the importance they attributed to information from farmers and extension agents in making agricultural research decisions. The indicators developed are listed in Table 6-2.

A review of the data in Table 6-2 pertaining to the frequency and perceived importance of researcher-extension agent contacts suggests that the organizational fusion of R & E bureaus meant very little in terms of institutionalizing an effective two-way communication channel between researchers and extension agents. The MEETRGO indicator showed that approximately 75% of both CORD and PORD scientists met with extension agents twice a year or less. Considering the fairly high rate at which scientists reported presenting lectures to extension worker audiences (RGOLEC), this seemed to reflect a low degree of informal, "collegial" information exchange. Only 14% and 17% of the CORD and PORD scientists, respectively,

TABLE 6-2. Clientele Influence Indicators (percent)

Approximately how often do you talk with the following people to share information about research in progress?

MEETRGO (21f)   Rural guidance staff (extension agents).

	CORD	PORD
Daily	0	0
Weekly	1	7
Monthly	22	18
Biannually	32	35
Rarely	45	40

MEETFARM (21g)   Farmers.

	CORD	PORD
Daily	1	3
Weekly	5	3
Monthly	22	28
Biannually	36	41
Rarely	36	26

During the past year have you participated in the following activities?

FARMLEC (23f)   Lectured at a meeting of farmers.

	CORD	PORD
Yes	45	62
No	55	38

RGOLEC (23g)   Lectured at a meeting of rural guidance workers.

	CORD	PORD
Yes	53	38
No	47	62

TABLE 6-2. Continued

FARMINFO (4)	It is easy for researchers at my institute to get accurate information about production problems at the farm level.

	CORD	PORD
Strongly agree	3	7
Agree	35	48
Uncertain	42	12
Disagree	19	33
Strongly disagree	3	0

RGOVIS (6)	It seems that rural guidance workers frequently come to our institute to obtain advice about technical agricultural problems.

	CORD	PORD
Strongly agree	27	10
Agree	65	62
Uncertain	7	12
Disagree	0	17
Strongly disagree	1	0

Rank the reasons for working on particular research projects:

FARMNEED (20b)   My assessment of farmers' needs.

	CORD	PORD
Very important	45	64
Somewhat important	42	33
Of little importance	12	3
Least important	1	0

FARMWANT (20f)   Discussions with farmers about their problems.

	CORD	PORD
Very important	60	64
Somewhat important	29	31
Of little importance	8	5
Least important	3	0

TABLE 6-2. Continued

RGOTALK (201)   Feedback from rural guidance workers.

	CORD	PORD
Very important	14	17
Somewhat important	50	48
Of little importance	23	23
Least important	14	12

Rank the following activity in terms of satisfaction.

FARMSOLV (28d)   Giving advice to a farmer about a technical agricultural problem.

	CORD	PORD
Much satisfaction	59	59
Some satisfaction	34	41
Least satisfaction	7	0

ranked feedback from extension workers as "very important" in research decisions (RGOTALK). When compared with the percentage of "very important" responses generated by other clientele influence indicators (e.g., FARMNEED—45% CORD, 64% PORD; FARMWANT—60% CORD, 64% PORD) and administrative authority indicators (e.g., ORDGOAL—39% CORD, 51% PORD) in this same ranking exercise, extension agent influence appeared weak. This lack of interest by researchers in what extension agents thought contrasted with the researchers' perceptions of extension agent interest in what was going on at the research station. In response to the statement "It seems that rural guidance workers frequently come to our institute to obtain advice about technical agricultural problems" (RGOVIS), 92% of CORD and 72% of PORD respondents "strongly agreed" or "agreed."

One possible reason for this apparent one-way flow of information is the divergent educational backgrounds of researchers and extension agents. Those ORD employees who have official status as researchers must have at least a baccalaureate degree and must pass the appropriate state civil service examination given by the Ministry of Agriculture. Many agricultural researchers have master's degrees, and an increasing number hold doctorates. The extension service, on the other hand, has experienced a continual erosion of educational qualifications among its field staff, with many now holding only high school certificates or at most credentials from two-year agricultural colleges. The eroding educational base of the extension agent corps is an acknowledged problem within the agrobureaucracy. The consequences are probably more serious in status conscious Korean society than they would be in other social settings. In Korea, educational credentialism often influences social interaction. In the ORD situation, researchers, in effect, may feel that they have little to learn from young, inexperienced extension agents who lack equivalent formal educational training. And extension agents may feel awkward in seeking out advice in informal settings from higher status researchers in ORD. While the ORD organizational structure unites research and extension under one administrative roof, communications are compartmentalized in chain-of-command fashion within the separate research and extension bureaus. The fact that extension field agents are, in effect, staff adjuncts to provincial and county governments further complicates the structure of effective communication channels and demands placed upon extension agents. Field agents may, in fact, spend most of their time implementing government policy, with systematic information gathering and user feedback activities deemphasized. Communications often take place in formal institutional planning sessions that bring researchers and extension agents together under proforma conditions. Much time is spent presenting official reports and briefings. These events have often been orchestrated to reinvigorate organizational commitment to state development goals, rather than to air problems in give-and-take fashion. Both the formal settings of these meetings and their objectives may have mitigated against effective sharing of information between working scientists and extension field agents.

What conclusions can be reached concerning farmer-research worker interaction? Several indicators show that researchers placed considerable stock in responding to farmers' wants (FARMWANT), assessing farmers' needs (FARMNEED), and helping farmers solve production problems (FARMSOLV). The rural background of many scientists accounts in part for this receptivity. Also, the ORD's official ideology of service to farmers is constantly reinforced in banners and sloganeering placed in prominent view at the research stations. Given the frequency with which researchers reported meeting with farmers, one has reservations about the degree of effective, spontaneous interaction between the two parties. Reported scientist contacts with farmers show that a sizeable majority (72% of CORD scientists, 67% of PORD scientists) met with farmers two times a year or less (MEETFARM). In addition, a substantial number of scientists (62% CORD, 45% PORD) were either uncertain about or not convinced that researchers at their institute were getting accurate information about production problems at the farm level (FARMINFO).

In summary, PORD scientists, expected to be in closer contact with farmers due to physical and social proximity and their applied research mandate, do not show significantly higher levels of interaction with their clientele than CORD colleagues. Frequency of contact measures (e.g., MEETRGO, MEETFARM) reveal no significant differences. Reiterating the fact that interest group activity among farmers was minimal during the period under consideration, the infrequency of contact between farmers and ORD researchers suggests an "articulation" problem.

Scientific Influence and ORD Scientist Behavior

The other potential power source tapped in the questionaire was scientific influence. In the parlance of sociologists, scientists internalize a reward system that encourages the production of new knowledge. Status within the scientific community is a function of recognition by one's peers of research contributions that are judged to be scientifically meaningful (i.e., contributions that expand the extant knowledge base within particular disciplines and/or problem areas). The increased appropriation of science by government through the public funding of research has produced tensions between the scientific community (oriented toward the intrinsic value of the scientific endeavor) and those who fund research ("laymen" oriented toward pragmatic applications). State-sponsored agricultural research organizations are by design results oriented, requiring accommodations between scientists, funding agents, and the end-user clientele. As mentioned earlier, it has been suggested that the hallmark of a developed agricultural research system is an effective internal division of labor generating complementary applied and basic scientific research activities, thus promoting a synergistic mix of clientele and scientific influence on research decision making.

Dependence on the funding side is offset, in part, by the ability of scientists to exclude laymen from their world. This situation occurs, of course, as a result of extended periods of formal education and apprenticeship during which the scientist develops mastery over a specialized body of knowledge. Social power is accumulated through the professionalization of scientific work (Rueschemeyer 1986). A high degree of control over the knowledge generating and translation processes resides within the scientific fraternity, providing potential organizational resources which can be deployed in intergroup struggles for social advantage. Whether this potential organizational power can be activated determines the outcome of scientific and clientele (including the state) bargaining over research agendas and priorities in publicly funded research organizations, and reveals much about existing state/society relationships.

Measuring the scientific influence concept was also relatively straightforward. Indicators of participation in formal scientific activities were selected—for example, publication of scientific papers and presentation of papers at scientific meetings; integration into the wider scientific community through membership in scientific organizations; and attitudes toward scientific values which influence work patterns. Scientific influence indicators are listed in Table 6-3.

A variety of attitudinal measures (PUBSAT, SCISOLVE, ENJOY, PUBLISH, CURIO) suggested that ORD scientists were effectively socialized into the world of science. However, the chapter on the Tongil rice development and diffusion campaign pointed to the inability of the scientific community to effectively raise its voice against the implementation of expedient technical measures supported by the highest ranking officials in the agrobureaucracy, who were taking their cues from the preferences of high-level state officials for expeditious rice self-sufficiency measures. Scientists presented technical arguments against the exclusive reliance on and rapid diffusion of the Tongil varietal type in rice self-sufficiency efforts. Yet their warnings were not heeded. The inability of scientists within ORD to override the Tongil juggernaut illustrated political weakness. Organizational insularity is noted in the survey data, as ORD scientists apparently found it difficult to reach across organizational boundaries. The indicators UNIVLEC and RINSTLEC, for example, revealed a lack of interorganizational networking which may be necessary to cultivate political support in intra- and interbureaucratic debates on

TABLE 6-3. Scientific Influence Indicators (percent)

Rank the following in terms of personal satisfaction:

PUBSAT (28a)   Publishing a paper in a scientific journal.

	CORD	PORD
Much satisfaction	57	74
Some satisfaction	37	21
Least satisfaction	5	5

SCISOLVE (27f)   Finding a solution to a complex scientific problem I have struggled with.

	CORD	PORD
Much satisfaction	75	65
Some satisfaction	21	20
Least satisfaction	4	15

Rank the importance of reasons for working on particular research projects:

ENJOY (20a)   Enjoy doing this kind of work.

	CORD	PORD
Very important	40	44
Somewhat important	44	37
Of little importance	14	17
Least important	1	2

PUBLISH (20e)   Good chance to publish results in scientific journal.

	CORD	PORD
Very important	10	24
Somewhat important	38	51
Of little importance	37	15
Least importance	15	10

CURIO (20g)   Scientific curiosity.

	CORD	PORD
Very important	29	24
Somewhat important	48	49
Of little importance	16	20
Least important	7	7

TABLE 6-3. Continued

UNIVLEC (23c)	Lectured at a college or university during the past year.	
	CORD	PORD
Yes	11	2
No	89	98

RINSTLEC (23d)	Lectured at another government research institute during the past year.	
	CORD	PORD
Yes	15	5
No	85	95

KMEETPAR (23a)	Attended a meeting of a Korean professional scientific society during the past year.	
	CORD	PORD
Yes	65	63
No	35	37

OFFICER (26c)	Have you ever been an officer in a Korean professional scientific society?	
	CORD	PORD
Yes	15	3
No	85	97

SUBKJ (27a)	Number of subscriptions to Korean professional scientific journals.	
	CORD	PORD
None	43	55
1	29	17
2	20	26
3+	8	2

policy. Only 11% of CORD and 2% of PORD scientists reported lecturing at a college or university during the past year; only 15% of CORD scientists and 5% of PORD scientists had lectured at a non-ORD government research institute.

Organizational weakness among the Korean scientific fraternity is revealed further in the data on participation in organized scientific activities and commitment to science as a profession. A substantial minority of ORD scientists (35% CORD; 37% PORD) did not attend a Korean professional society meeting during the past year (KMEETPAR). A significant number (roughly half) of ORD scientists did not subscribe to a Korean professional society journal (SUBKJ). In addition, few ORD scientists have served in official capacities in Korean professional scientific organizations (OFFICER).

The perception (see STATUS, item 12, in Appendix 6-A) among a vast majority of ORD scientists that university scientists enjoy higher social prestige within the Korean scientific community may be a barrier to organizational and political cohesion, thus making scientific influence a less important factor in research decision making. Unfortunately, this social distinction is institutionalized materially via significant pay differentials between scientists with university appointments and ORD research workers. This salary differential reinforces feelings of status distinction within the Korean scientific community and fosters resentment among ORD ranks, making scientific cooperation and mutual interest association more difficult.

It is important to note that scientific interaction patterns within the system as a whole appear to be suboptimal.[2] There are annual systemwide planning and evaluation sessions that all scientists attend. The indicators of scientific communication may be skewed upward by the reporting of these meetings as scientifically meaningful interactions, but these meetings often do not represent important substantive inputs into a scientist's work. Rather, they function to reinforce ORD organizational goals in a public setting.

Perhaps weak scientific ties can be explained partially by weakness in national science education and training programs. Capable scientists may have few prospective collaborators. Approximately one-half of scientist respondents agreed or strongly agreed with the statement that they "felt frustrated because of the lack of good colleagues to work with in their institute" (COLFRUS, item 15, Appendix 6-A). Also important are the administrative demands on working time noted earlier (TADM, Table 6-1). In an agricultural research organization where other responsibilities such as extension and/or teaching are not imposed on scientists, this represents an inordinate drain on the researcher's time and limits the amount of interaction with the wider scientific community. In informal in-depth interviews, many scientists complained of the official report writing and other administrative duties that distracted them from more productive work.

In summary, CORD scientists, as expected due to their higher educational levels, had somewhat higher scores on professional interaction variables (e.g., UNIVLEC, RINTSLEC, OFFICER, SUBKJ) than PORD colleagues. The participation rates were often quite low, however. These results suggest that ORD scientists have difficulty acting as a unified professional interest group to advance their own agendas within the agrobureaucracy. Attitudinal measures showed strong orientations toward scientific values among both groups of scientists, but these values seem to have been weakly articulated in an effective organizational sense.

Summing Up: Authority, Influence, and the ORD Division of Labor

As stated previously, the weights of scientific influence, clientele influence, and administrative authority on research decision making within ORD should be analyzed by factoring in expected CORD-PORD differences based on the division of labor within the organization. Work on local level adaptation problems at the PORD sites should require a tight, self-contained research network within the institute, with research directors and supervisors receiving instructions from CORD units about new technologies and information from regional government units about clientele responses to agricultural production problems. In effect, the job of the PORD scientist is to verify the appropriateness of newly developed CORD technologies and/or to modify them for regional diffusion. The concrete nature of the task and the rather direct theoretical accountability of PORD units to CORD research programs, provincial government agencies, and a farmer clientele should support an inner-directed research communication and cooperation network. In contrast, at the CORDs, where more basic research tasks are emphasized, the need to extend the scientist's research communication and collaboration networks beyond his/her own institute seems apparent. CORD scientists at other institutes and university scientists with similar research interests become necessary collaborators in an effective CORD research program. The emphasis is on the *relative frequency* of intra- and interinstitute research communication and collaboration patterns. A well-functioning research system would promote a significant number of meaningful external professional contacts among both CORD and PORD scientists. To see if these differential patterns of research communication and cooperation were developed, PORD and CORD scientists were asked about their interactions with four relevant sets of actors: the scientist's institute director and research supervisor, colleagues within the same institute, ORD scientists at other institutes, and university professors (most likely university scientists who have joint research appointments with ORD).

Indicators of communication patterns are listed in Table 6-4. When researchers were asked how often they shared information about research-in-progress with different colleague cohorts, the hypothesized CORD-PORD communication patterns outlined above were only weakly substantiated. Communication within the institute greatly overshadowed external communications in both researcher subgroups. Collegial research communications within the institute (MEETCOLL) were slightly more frequent for CORD than for PORD researchers, with 83% of CORD researchers reporting at least weekly interaction with institute colleagues compared to 76% of PORD respondents. Supervisory communication patterns, on the other hand, were slightly more important for PORD researchers. Among the PORD subgroup, 89% of the sample reported at least weekly communications with their immediate supervisor (MEETSUP), compared to 78% of the CORD scientists. Communication with institute directors (MEETDIR) was far less frequent. A majority of PORD researchers (56%) communicated with their institute director at least monthly, while 43% of CORD researchers reported the same frequency of research communication.

External communication occurred much less frequently. Collegial interaction with ORD researchers in other institutes was reported to occur at least monthly by 28% of CORD scientists and 12% of PORD researchers (MEETORD). On the other hand, 37% of the PORD scientists reported communicating

TABLE 6-4. ORD Scientist Communication Patterns (percent)

Approximately how often do you talk with the following people to share information about research in progress?

MEETCOLL (21a)   Co-worker at my institute.

	CORD	PORD
Daily	50	56
Weekly	33	20
Monthly	12	7
Biannually	4	15
Rarely	1	2

MEETDIR (21b)   Director of my institute.

	CORD	PORD
Daily	5	7
Weekly	14	20
Monthly	24	29
Biannually	22	24
Rarely	34	20

MEETSUP (21c)   Chief of my section.

	CORD	PORD
Daily	35	37
Weekly	43	52
Monthly	21	8
Biannually	1	3
Rarely	0	0

MEETORD (21d)   ORD researchers at other institutes.

	CORD	PORD
Daily	0	0
Weekly	3	2
Monthly	25	10
Biannually	53	68
Rarely	19	20

TABLE 6-4. Continued

MEETPROF (21e)   University professors.

	CORD	PORD
Daily	0	0
Weekly	1	2
Monthly	28	35
Biannually	45	43
Rarely	26	20

at least monthly with university scientists (MEETPROF), compared to 29% of CORD researchers.

Actual participation in cooperative research projects is reported in Table 6-5. Institutional differences in collaborative research patterns were not marked. The largest difference between CORD and PORD responses was reported for cooperative research with scientists in one's own institute (COOPCOLL), with 53% of CORD and 43% of PORD researchers reporting involvement in intrainstitute cooperative research projects. Research collaboration outside the scientist's own institute was far less common. Cooperative projects with researchers at another ORD institute (COOPORD) were reported by 22% of CORD and 14% of PORD scientists. PORD scientists, on the other hand, were more likely to participate in cooperative research with university scientists (COOPPROF); 21% of PORD compared to 16% of CORD respondents.

The data in Tables 6-4 and 6-5 do not reveal strongly differentiated patterns of research communication and cooperation based on an intraorganizational basic/applied scientific division of labor. When combined with previous data on clientele and scientific influence patterns analyzed earlier, it appears that ORD institutes were not able to institutionalize robust external channels of information and support. The inner-directed (within institute) communication and cooperation patterns which typify both CORD and PORD scientist responses attest to the strong administrative response capacity within ORD (recall indicators ORDGOAL and BOSS in Table 6-1). The ORD political environment was not conducive to the emergence of balanced, complementary power relationships within the research system (strong scientific influence patterns) or between the research system and relevant actors in the agricultural sector

TABLE 6-5. Scientific Cooperation Indicators (percent)

With whom did you cooperate when engaged in a cooperative research project?

COOPCOLL (17c)   Researchers at your institute.

	CORD	PORD
Yes	53	43
No	47	57

COOPORD (17d)   Researchers at another ORD institute.

	CORD	PORD
Yes	22	14
No	78	86

COOPPROF (17e)   University scientists.

	CORD	PORD
Yes	16	21
No	84	79

(clientele influence). The CORD-PORD functional division of labor was based on principles of deconcentration that increased administrative responsiveness, rather than on principles of decentralization that facilitated societal responsiveness.

If one reflects on the Korean rice varietal development program discussed in Chapter 4, empirical indicators of scientific communication and cooperation patterns presented in this chapter support the earlier story about the forces behind the Tongil campaign. Strong state administrative pressures for rice self-sufficiency activated the Tongil research and diffusion program. Clientele pressures were weak, especially at the PORD institutes where one expected them to be strongest. The survey data reveal a paucity of communication links between researchers and farmers and between researchers and extension agents in ORD organizational life. Farmers' ambivalence about the Tongil diffusion program was certainly justified, given their apparent lack of input into the R & D process. The robustness of scientific influence within the organization was also problematic and helps to explain the inability of scientists to mount an effective challenge to the Tongil campaign on scientific/technical grounds.

In-depth interviews with ORD scientists and institute administrators reinforced this interpretation (see Appendix 6-B for a description of these interviews). Institute directors complained of their inability to adjust research programs in directions that reflected either influence from scientists or clientele. Institute directors, for example, did not have the latitude to shift resources (funding or personnel) between research projects based on their judgments of potential contributions to scientific understanding and/or clientele problem solving. Individual institute budgets and personnel allocations were, of course, passed down administratively reflecting MAF priorities in Seoul (and MAF often had to make significant budgetary concessions to the EPB). Sporadic local (provincial) research initiatives were effected through projects funded directly by the provincial governor. Of course, these administrative demands received priority attention, even if they disrupted ongoing programs and were of questionable relevance to regional agricultural production possibilities. The image is not one of the scientist-administrator who is able to reconcile bureaucratic demands with the agenda of a dynamic scientific community. Rather, the stereotypical conflict between bureaucratic rigidity and scientific flexibility seemed especially pronounced when talking with institute administrators about their inability to fend off bureaucratic pressures in the management of their research programs.

Hard State, Flexible Response?

How can a "hard state" manuever with the dexterity shown by Korean policymakers during the last two decades? A centralized, top-down mode of decision making and implementation seems antithetical to the administrative flexibility necessary for managing rapid social change internally while simultaneously maintaining a steadfast course in turbulent international economic waters. Effective state-proffered incentives to the private sector, movement rapidly up the industrial product cycle ladder, and swift adjustment to the oil shocks of the 1970s all characterize recent Korean economic history. If "administrative guidance" is the rule in the Korean political economy, flexibility rather than rigidity would seem to mark relations between the state sector and the private sector. How does one explain the preceding analysis of agricultural research policy in this context?

Michell (1984) contends that the emphasis on centralization, hierarchy, and command in the analyses of state-led growth in Korea is overdrawn. He counters with the following interpretation of bureaucratic decision making in Korea:

> There are four processes of decision making in action simultaneously within the formal, i.e., central government structure:
>
> 1. a hierarchical structure, in which decisions are made at the top (the process normally described);
> 2. a reverse hierarchy in which decisions are made at the bottom [lower bureaucratic ranks—Michell singles out the Assistant Director or grade 4 level] and validated at more senior levels;
> 3. an anarchic war of all against all in which conflicting decisions are made at all levels with strong competition between ministries;
> 4. competing with the formal decision making process is an informal one, which draws on traditional values of a face to face society, the rule of men rather than the rule of law [Kim Bun-woong 1982]. (Michell 1984:14)

According to Michell, process 1 is the usual interpretation of state intervention. However, processes 2-4 suggest that "voice," in Hirschman's (1970) terms, is heard and acted upon in substantive bureaucratic planning and implementation activities. Processes 2 and 3 ensure that regional and/or interbureaucratic interests are represented; process 4 is the main avenue for articulation of societal interests. Thus, the paucity of private associations or interest groups does not mean that important private interests are ignored in administrative circles.

Dore (1982:14) claims that in Korea, much like in Japan, policy decisions reflect an informal state/society consensus between the major players—an illustration he cites is the agreement between the government, banks, and industry over credit rationing. The informal interorganizational nexus in post-Confucian societies, which often crosscuts formal bureaucratic and private/public sector realms, is formed through social interlocks, principally school, family, and/or regional ties.

Group solidarity also extends into the bureaucratic ranks. Michell (1984) notes, for example, that identification with a particular ministry (MCI, Ministry of Commerce and Industry) or agency (EPB, Economic Planning Board) carries the same badge of occupational prestige and corporate identity as marks MOF (Ministry of Finance) or MITI (Ministry of International Trade and Industry) employees in Japan (Johnson 1982). The corporate character of the prestigious bureaucracies is based on the academic obstacle course that candidates must negotiate. School ties and similar trials of "examination hell" reinforce social solidarity among the initiated. Administrative guidance is effective in the East Asian context because bureaucratic recruitment is meritocratic (Steinberg 1985), again a legacy of scholar-official social domination in the premodern Confucian period. Not only does the education and examination system of such credential societies produce a competent, cohesive cadre of state officials, but the specter of bureaucratic corruption and associated kleptocratic decline seen in many authoritarian polities is forestalled to a degree by the meritocratic and social service ideology (rule by virtue) embedded in Confucian political culture (Pye 1985) (although a crosschecking interbureaucratic policing capacity provides a structural basis for periodic anticorruption house cleaning measures [Burmeister 1987b]).

Michell (1984) acknowledges, however, that certain sectors and strategic policy initiatives have been subjected to a more centralized, authoritative mode of planning and implementation than his bureaucratic model suggests. He explicitly cites agriculture and agricultural policy initiatives as illustrations of "hard state" bureaucratic rigidity. The reasons for this "special" treatment are both structural and historical. During the Japanese colonial period in Korea, authorities faced the difficult dilemma of expanding rice production for the Japanese homeland through the transformation of production relations in a subsistence-oriented, densely populated agrarian society. When the agrarian overlords were hated foreign interlopers, "accommodations" were possible only through coercion. A division of labor emerged within the agrobureaucracy to accomplish the dual objectives of increasing production and extracting the surplus, with a research organization similar to ORD responsible for technology development and a strong interior ministry (analogue to the present MHA) responsible for implementation of "rural development" programs, including diffusion of new agricultural technologies and foodgrain collection to meet colonial government procurement targets. The MHA's police powers were always at the disposal of local authorities if recalcitrant peasants objected on either front. Technology development was divorced organizationally from technology diffusion in a telling fashion, in effect severing an important feedback loop between the users and the producers of new technologies. In the earlier review of colonial history in Korea, it was noted that the interior ministry ruled by military authority in what was basically occupied territory.

After independence, the agrobureaucratic apparatus remained in place, largely for social control reasons. In the post-land reform era, peasant producers could withdraw into the subsistence production mode if threatened by state confiscatory policies. Again, MHA cadres had to be called out to oversee grain solicitations required to meet state procurement targets, alienating farmers. To deal with this problem, MHA powers were consolidated in the early 1960s when President Park abolished elected local government councils. The powerful MHA confronted an atomized, powerless mass of small landholder "clients." Effective informal networks of state official/private sector decision making could not form between agriculture as an interest and the agrobureaucracy in the same way as they did between industrial groups and the relevant ministries such as MCI because of the social imbalance of the relationship. There can be no quid pro quo when one side has nothing to give or to withhold. There were no captains of agriculture analogous to emerging captains of industry who could be drawn into informal policymaking networks where both parties could engage in meaningful (both sides had significant resource bases) give-and-take bargaining over the details of state-crafted initiatives designed to steer the private sector in directions congruent with state preferences. The "socially connected" rural aristocracy had moved from the countryside, leaving an amorphous mass of peasant farmers. As in the case of labor, unauthorized collective organization was proscribed in fact, if not in law, for political and economic control reasons. The agrarian power structure (or lack of such) did not lend itself to the type of informal negotiation between bureaucrats and private powerbrokers as envisioned by Michell (1984).

Jacobs (1985) views the Korean bureaucratic structure as the precipitate of an overarching patrimonial social order that continues to infuse all social relationships in Korean society. While his sweeping argument simplifies a very complex reality, he points to an important syncretism in Korean society—a modern state apparatus (strengthened to an extraordinary degree by the colonial experience and war—the state of siege has continued uninterrupted over several generations) superimposed upon traditional patterns of social organization. According to Jacobs, the state-rural sector relationship, in particular, takes on a prebendal flavor. Government largesse—improved technologies, NACF credit, fertilizer, more favorable terms of trade, etc.—is extended to the rural sector in return for plebisicitary political support and for cooperation in government mobilization campaigns to integrate the agricultural sector into the national economy on terms that facilitate a macroeconomic accommodation. This is not a contractual relationship, an exchange of government benefits for active support in a competitive political arena. Rather it is an episodic stipend or grant bestowed upon subjects by state officials. Acceptance/nonacceptance is the only reactive option available to those on the receiving end. This unbalanced, dependent social relationship can take on the attributes of a positive sum game. Earlier, in the Tongil discussion, we saw how the government in effect offered higher prices for farmer cultivation of high-yielding, lower-quality rice.

The definitive sociological study of the Korean bureaucracy remains to be written. The point stressed here is that our findings with regard to ORD decision making do not contradict Michell's more sophisticated argument about how the state and the interests coordinate flexible economic initiatives. Social characteristics of the Korean bureaucracy are sector-specific. Different possibilities exist for state manipulation and societal influence, depending on the structural characteristics of the affected subpopulation of "clients" and the historical legacies of particular agencies or ministries. The social cohesion that Michell claims infuses EPB and MCI is not as evident in the agricultural bureaucracies. The MAF has traditionally been a weak ministry, as evidenced by low agricultural sector budgetary allocations (Ban 1985:98). The bulk of government investment in agriculture, in turn, has been allocated to infrastructural projects (land reclamation and irrigation) in which oversight and implementation either fall upon the Ministry of Construction or the Agricultural Development Corporation (a semiautonomous public corporation), both prime bureaucratic slots for retired military officers given their large budgets and activist, mobilization bent. A telling statistic regarding social cohesiveness within ORD was the WORKPLAN indicator (item 13, Appendix 6-A) in the scientist survey. Less than one-half of ORD scientist respondents answered either "strongly agree" or "agree" to the following statement: "Five years from now I plan to be working for ORD." This apparent lack of commitment to a career in the organization is not conducive to waging strong interbureaucratic battles of turf and/or successfully coopting private sector support through informal channels. Current ORD problems with scientist attrition (movement to academia) reflect this lack of cohesion within the organization.

The issues broached in this last section only begin to suggest the type of inquiry that is required to understand how the Korean bureaucracy works. Case studies of decision making within different bureaucracies are required. These studies must eventually be collated to arrive at a clearer picture of the power relationships that condition bureaucratic initiative and response. Historical, comparative sociological methods must be deployed alongside survey research and other formal data collection instruments. In this study we have emphasized social structural determinants of bureaucratic organization and activity, looking at both internal and external political and economic conditions which have generated the primacy of the state and its bureaucratic organs within the state/society relationship. A more complete explanation requires a synthesis between interpretations based on social structure and political culture (see Pye 1985; Kim, Bell, and Lee 1985). Pye's (1985) recent discussion of distinctive Asian conceptualizations of power and the implications of these political cultures for concrete political structures and state/society relationships require careful consideration in any future explanatory synthesis. This is a formidable research agenda, at both the theoretical and empirical levels.

Notes

1. Specific questions in the questionnaire are cited in this chapter using a capitalized code designation, e.g., FRESULT. The questionnaire is reproduced in its entirety in Appendix 6-A at the end of this chapter. Perusal of the entire questionnaire will put the comparisons and ranking dimensions of the indicators in a more focused context. We have extracted specific indicators from the questionnaire to provide empirical support for points made about the relative importance of administrative authority, scientific influence, and clientele influence in the ORD organizational life.

2. Details on how additional information was solicited from researchers, research administrators, farmers, and extension agents are provided in Appendix 6-B at the end of this chapter.

APPENDIX 6-A: SURVEY QUESTIONNAIRE

Sampling Procedures

The sample population consisted of all ORD employees classified as research scientists. Directors and department heads (research section chiefs) were excluded from this population due to questions about the amount of time they were expected to devote to research. When possible, in-depth, open-ended interviews were conducted with this group. From among a population of roughly 600 scientists (as classified by ORD civil service rank), the self-administered questionnaire was distributed to 118 respondents (about 20% of the target population). Using a random numbers table, scientists were randomly selected from each institute visited (7 of 9 provincial research institutes and 9 of 13 specialized central institutes) with numbers from each institute proportional to the institute's percentage of the total ORD scientist population. In a few cases due to absence or other prior commitments, substitutions for randomly selected scientists were made, but these isolated cases should not affect the overall random properties of the sample.

Questionnaire Pretest

Prior to administration of the survey questionnaires, pretests were conducted at one provincial research institute and one specialized research institute in order to check response time, problems with question interpretation, and adequacy of directions for answering questionnaire items. The pretest provided assurances that the questionnaire could be completed by the respondents in a reasonable amount of time (45 minutes to one hour), and that questions and response categories were understood by the target groups.

Administrative Details

The questionnaires were translated into Korean for administration. The strategy of administration was to ask all randomly selected respondents at each institute to fill out the questionnaire at the same time in order to minimize respondent consultation and to collect all questionnaires promptly after they were completed in order to prevent their possible misuse by administrators. This was possible in all but two cases where, due to events beyond our control, we were forced to distribute questionnaires one day and pick them up at a later time.

Adapting the Questionnaire to the Environment

As Aqua (1974) has observed, the organizational life in the Korean bureaucracy provides, on occasion, an "intense experience" for those directly involved. Prior to the period of fieldwork (July, 1981-September, 1982), there had been several shake-ups in the bureaucracy following the gradual ascendancy of General Chun Doo-Hwan after the October, 1979, assassination of President Park Chung-Hee. The political situation within the bureaucracy was still uncertain. This factor, combined with other characteristics of the bureaucratic culture in Korea, explains the rather conservative nature of the survey instrument—in other words, some indirect methods of gaining information about sensitive political problems within the organization had to be employed. The result is a very imperfect instrument. In-depth interviews with actors both inside and outside of the organization were used to augment information obtained from the survey questionnaires. Yet, there remains, in the phrase of the methodologists, a lot of error in the variables. These errors are, unfortunately, a fact of life in obtaining data on sensitive topics and are especially likely in cross-cultural research. Multimethod research strategies are required to check the accuracy of various sources of information.

Survey Questionnaire

The questions cited below were asked of the previously described random stratified sample of agricultural scientists employed by the Office of Rural Development during 1981-1982. Following each question, questionnaire response totals are reported. The number preceding the equals sign is the response category code (e.g., 1 = strongly agree, etc.). Two numbers follow the equals sign. The first number is the total number of respondents whose answer corresponded to the specified response category. The number in parentheses is the subtotal for the central research institutes (CORDs).

Please read the following statements and circle the response which best indicates your feeling:
1 = Strongly agree; 2 = Agree; 3 = Uncertain; 4 = Disagree; 5 = Strongly disagree.

1. FRESULT   I have much freedom to interpret research results.
   1 = 23(14); 2 = 57(41); 3 = 21(11); 4 = 14(7); 5 = 2(2)

2. COOPPART   If I spend time working outside my institute on cooperative projects, it will be difficult for me to complete my work assignments.
   1 = 26(15); 2 = 44(30); 3 = 17(8); 4 = 25(18); 5 = 5(4)

3. EQUIPUSE   It is easy for me to use research equipment at another institute for my own research.
   1 = 2(1); 2 = 18(7); 3 = 57(42); 4 = 39(25); 5 = 1(0)

4. FARMINFO   It is easy for researchers at my institute to get accurate information about production problems at the farm level.
   1 = 5(2); 2 = 46(26); 3 = 36(31); 4 = 28(14); 5 = 2(2)

5. SCIADMR   The relationship between scientists and administrators at our institute is more collegial than supervisory.
   1 = 2(0); 2 = 25(17); 3 = 24(18); 4 = 47(27); 5 = 19(13)

6. RGOVIS   It seems that rural guidance workers frequently come to our institute to obtain advice about technical agricultural problems.
   1 = 24(20); 2 = 75(49); 3 = 10(5); 4 = 7(0); 5 = 1(1)

7. FTOPIC   I have a reasonable amount of freedom to choose my own research topics.
   1 = 22(6); 2 = 54(36); 3 = 27(22); 4 = 13(10); 5 = 1(1)

8. EDOP   The educational opportunities offered by ORD provide good chances for the researcher to increase occupational prestige.
    1 = 7(3); 2 = 17(12); 3 = 41(31);
    4 = 41(21); 5 = 10(7)

9. FUTUREAD   In the future if the opportunity arises, I plan to move from research to administration.
    1 = 6(5); 2 = 12(10); 3 = 19(8);
    4 = 38(25); 5 = 42(27)

10. WORKQUAL   Within ORD it is difficult for scientists to achieve recognition based on the quality of their work.
    1 = 7(4); 2 = 33(23); 3 = 29(20);
    4 = 44(26); 5 = 4(2)

11. MULDISOP   If a scientist wants to advance in ORD, it is better to focus one's attention on work within the institute rather than to participate in multi-disciplinary research with other institutes.
    1 = 10(9); 2 = 37(20); 3 = 27(20);
    4 = 34(21); 5 = 9(5)

12. STATUS   Within the Korean scientific community, the status of the university scientist is higher than that of the ORD scientist.
    1 = 84(57); 2 = 26(15); 3 = 2(2);
    4 = 0; 5 = 5(2)

13. WORKPLAN   Five years from now I plan to be working for ORD.
    1 = 20(10); 2 = 27(17); 3 = 58(38);
    4 = 10(9); 5 = 3(2)

14. GOALUNCE   Uncertainty about the future of Korean agriculture makes it difficult for my institute to focus on research goals.
    1 = 7(6); 2 = 32(18); 3 = 13(10);
    4 = 51(30); 5 = 17(11)

15. COLFRUS I often feel frustrated because of the lack of good colleagues to work with in my institute.
    1 = 11(8); 2 = 45(28); 3 = 5(4);
    4 = 51(33); 5 = 6(3)

16. In the course of a year, please estimate the percentage of time spent during work hours on the following activities:

    a. TRES Laboratory and/or field research.
        0-20 = 13(9); 21-40 = 43(30); 41-60 = 43(26);
        61-80 = 15(8); 81+ = 3(3)
    b. TLIBR Library research.
        0-5 = 37(22); 6-10 = 48(32);
        11-20 = 25(18); 21+ = 7(4)
    c. TADM Administrative tasks (filling out official forms and writing official reports).
        0-10 = 22(16); 11-20 = 34(21); 21-30 = 30(15);
        31+ = 31(24)
    d. TMEETING Conferences and meetings.
        0-5 = 76(50); 6-10 = 33(18); 11+ = 8(8)
    e. OTHER Other (specify).
        0-5 = 65(43); 6-10 = 25(18); 11+ = 27(15)

17. a. RPROJNO During the past year how many research projects did you work on?
        0 = 24(12); 1 = 34(23); 2 = 23(14);
        3 = 17(12); 4+ = 17(12)
    b. COOPPRNO Among these projects, how many were done cooperatively with other researchers?
        0-1 = 58(35); 2-3 = 40(26); 4+ = 20(12)
        With whom did you cooperate?
    c. COOPCOLL Researchers at your institute.
        Yes = 58(40); No = 60(36)
    d. COOPORD Researchers at another ORD institute.
        Yes = 23(17); No = 95(59)
    e. COOPPROF University scientist.
        Yes = 21(12); No = 97(64)
    f. COOPGOV Researchers at other government institutes.
        Yes = 3(3); No = 115(73)

18. a. FIVEYR   Have you worked in basically the same research position for over five years?
       Yes = 80(53);   No = 35(23)
    b. WORKLOAD   If yes, think back to past years. Has the number of projects you have worked on:
       Increased? 35(19)
       Remained about the same? 45(33)
       Decreased? 1(1)

19. Please rank the importance of each of the following items to ORD performance:
       1 = Very important;
       2 = Somewhat important;
       3 = Least important.

    a. FACILITY   Lack of adequate research facilities.
       1 = 72(40); 2 = 32(26); 3 = 9(7)
    b. RESFUND   Lack of adequate project funds.
       1 = 48(32); 2 = 51(30); 3 = 11(8)
    c. MANPOWER   Inadequate scientific manpower.
       1 = 59(40); 2 = 39(23); 3 = 14(10)
    d. AMPRESS   Bad research atmosphere due to administrative pressures.
       1 = 62(34); 2 = 42(33); 3 = 5(2)
    e. PROMO   Lack of promotion opportunities for working scientists.
       1 = 52(37); 2 = 26(24); 3 = 11(11)
    f. LACKCOOP   Lack of opportunities for cooperation with scientists at other institutes.
       1 = 22(15); 2 = 46(39); 3 = 16(14)
    g. LOWPAY   Low pay scale compared to skills required.
       1 = 94(58); 2 = 20(15); 3 = 3(3)

20. Think about the current or recently completed research projects on which you have worked. Please rank the importance of each of the following reasons for working on particular research projects.
       1 = Very important;
       2 = Somewhat important;
       3 = Of little importance;
       4 = Least important.

a. ENJOY   Enjoy doing this kind of research.
   1 = 46(28); 2 = 46(31); 3 = 17(10); 4 = 2(1)
b. FARMNEED   My assessment of farmers' needs.
   1 = 58(31); 2 = 43(29); 3 = 9(8); 4 = 1(1)
c. FUNDING   Availability of research funds.
   1 = 2(1); 2 = 14(9); 3 = 35(18); 4 = 59(41)
d. BOSS   Assignment by my superior.
   1 = 16(7); 2 = 59(42); 3 = 29(17); 4 = 8(5)
e. PUBLISH   Good chance to publish results in a scientific journal.
   1 = 17(7); 2 = 47(26); 3 = 31(25); 4 = 14(10)
f. FARMWANT   Discussions with farmers about their problems.
   1 = 70(43); 2 = 34(21); 3 = 8(6); 4 = 2(2)
g. CURIO   Scientific curiosity.
   1 = 30(20); 2 = 53(33); 3 = 19(11); 4 = 8(5)
h. TIMING   Ability to complete the research within a limited amount of time.
   1 = 11(3); 2 = 31(22); 3 = 38(24); 4 = 30(21)
i. COLLHELP   Assist colleagues working in a related area.
   1 = 9(5); 2 = 51(32); 3 = 39(28); 4 = 12(6)
j. ORDGOAL   Direct relationship with ORD goals for agricultural development.
   1 = 50(29); 2 = 53(38); 3 = 9(6); 4 = 3(1)
k. TOOLS   Availability of research facilities.
   1 = 7(4); 2 = 28(12); 3 = 46(31); 4 = 28(22)
l. RGOTALK   Feedback from rural guidance (extension) workers.
   1 = 16(9); 2 = 52(33); 3 = 24(15); 4 = 14(9)

21. Approximately how often do you talk with the following people to share information about research in progress?
   1 = Daily; 2 = Weekly; 3 = Monthly;
   4 = Biannually; 5 = Rarely.

a. MEETCOLL   Co-workers at my institute.
   1 = 61(38); 2 = 33(25); 3 = 12(9);
   4 = 9(3); 5 = 2(1)
b. MEETDIR   Director of my institute.
   1 = 7(4); 2 = 19(11); 3 = 30(18);
   4 = 27(17); 5 = 34(26)

c. MEETSUP Chief of my section.
   1 = 41(26); 2 = 53(32); 3 = 19(16);
   4 = 2(1); 5 = 0
d. MEETORD ORD researchers at other institutes.
   1 = 0; 2 = 3(2); 3 = 23(19);
   4 = 68(40); 5 = 22(14)
e. MEETPROF University professors.
   1 = 0; 2 = 2(1); 3 = 35(21);
   4 = 50(33); 5 = 27(19)
f. MEETRGO Rural guidance staff.
   1 = 0; 2 = 4(1); 3 = 23(16);
   4 = 38(24); 5 = 49(33)
g. MEETFARM Farmers.
   1 = 2(1); 2 = 5(4); 3 = 27(16);
   4 = 42(26); 5 = 36(26)
h. MEETGOV Government officials outside ORD.
   1 = 0; 2 = 0; 3 = 3(1); 4 = 21(16);
   5 = 88(57)

22. Scientists often need technical advice when working on a difficult problem. Among the following persons, who would you ask for advice?
    1 = Most likely;
    2 = Possibly;
    3 = Least likely.

    a. OTHERHEL Fellow scientist at another institute.
       1 = 49(37); 2 = 59(33); 3 = 7(4)
    b. DIRHELP Director of my institute.
       1 = 29(18); 2 = 45(28); 3 = 37(25)
    c. SUPHELP My research section chief.
       1 = 52(38); 2 = 56(35); 3 = 7(2)
    d. OWNHELP Co-worker at my institute.
       1 = 30(19); 2 = 58(36); 3 = 26(20)

23. During the past year have you participated in the following activities?

    a. KMEETPAR Attended a meeting of a Korean professional scientific society.
       Yes = 76(49); No = 41(26)

b. KPUB   Presented a paper at a Korean professional scientific meeting.
   Yes = 48(33); No = 68(41)
c. UNIVLEC   Lectured at a college or university.
   Yes = 9(8); No = 107(66)
d. RINSTLEC   Lectured at another government research institute.
   Yes = 13(11); No = 102(62)
e. GINSTLEC   Lectured at another government agency (non-research).
   Yes = 28(18); No = 88(56)
f. FARMLEC   Lectured at a meeting of farmers.
   Yes = 57(33); No = 59(41)
g. RGOLEC   Lectured at a meeting of rural guidance workers.
   Yes = 55(39); No = 61(35)

24. During the past five years have you participated in the following scientific activities?

    a. INTMPART   Attended an international scientific conference.
       Yes = 23(17); No = 94(58)
    b. INTPUB   Presented a paper at an international scientific conference.
       Yes = 12(12); No = 105(63)

25. How many papers have you published in Korean scientific journals over the

    a. YRPUB   Past year?
       0 = 72(40); 1 = 26(18); 2+ = 20(18)
    b. PASTPUB   Past five years?
       0 = 45(20); 1 = 15(9); 2 = 16(11);
       3 = 13(11); 4+ = 27(23)

26. What professional societies do you belong to?

    a. KSOCMEM   Korean professional societies.
       0 = 17(10); 1 = 65(40); 2 = 30(22); 3+ = 6(4)
    b. ISOCMEM   International scientific societies.
       0 = 115(73); 1 = 3(3)

c. OFFICER   Have you ever been an officer in one of these societies?
Yes = 12(11); No = 101(63)

27. What professional journals do you subscribe to?

   a. SUBKJ   Korean.
      0 = 56(33); 1 = 29(22); 2 = 26(15); 3+ = 7(6)
   b. SUBIJ   Foreign.
      0 = 65(36); 1 = 17(13); 2 = 21(15);
      3+ = 15(12)

28. Please rank each of the following activities in terms of the personal satisfaction you derive from them.
      1 = Much satisfaction;
      2 = Some satisfaction;
      3 = Least satisfaction.

   a. PUBSAT   Publishing a paper in a scientific journal.
      1 = 72(42); 2 = 36(28); 3 = 6(4)
   b. TIMESAT   Completing my research projects on schedule.
      1 = 75(52); 2 = 36(17); 3 = 5(5)
   c. COOPSAT   Helping a colleague with a scientific problem.
      1 = 41(28); 2 = 63(36); 3 = 9(8)
   d. FARMSOLV   Giving advice to a farmer about a technical agricultural problem.
      1 = 67(43); 2 = 42(25); 3 = 5(5)
   e. PLANSAT   Taking part in discussions about future research programs at the institute.
      1 = 44(24); 2 = 56(36); 3 = 11(10)
   f. SCISOLV   Finding a solution to a complex scientific problem that I have struggled with.
      1 = 81(55); 2 = 23(15); 3 = 9(3)

The following items refer to personal background information. A few questions were not coded because the data was not used directly in the analysis.

29.   AGE   Age of respondent.
         Mean = 37(37)

30. Educational background.
    a. UNIVED   Type of degree
       BA = 54(29); MS = 39(28); PHD = 12(12)
    b. AREASTUD   Major field.
       (Data not coded.)
    c. PASTGRAD   Year of graduation.
       (Data not coded.)

31. EDMATCH   If you have received graduate training, what were your areas of specialization?
    (Data not coded.)

32. What is your current area of research specialization at ORD?   (Data not coded.)

33. ORD employment history:

    a. YEARSERV   Date at which you started work.
       Mean years of service = 10(11)
    b. ENTGRADE   Rank at the time you started work.
       (Data not coded.)
    c. NOWGRADE   Present rank.
       (Data not coded.)
    d. PROMONUM   Number of promotions.
       0 = 10(2); 1 = 36(26); 2 = 19(18); 3+ = 2(2)
    e. OTHERSER   Other institutions within ORD for which you have worked.
       0 = 79(49); 1 = 21(18); 2+ = 6(6);
       RGO = 10(3)

34. Have you received special educational training after you started working for ORD?

    a. OVERGRAD   Graduate degree at a foreign university.
       Yes = 9(8); No = 104(66)
    b. LONGOTR   Long-term overseas training.
       Yes = 22(16); No = 91(58)
    c. SHORTOTR   Short-term overseas training.
       Yes = 20(18); No = 93(56)
    d. LDOMTR   Long-term domestic training.
       Yes = 4(4); No = 109(70)
    e. SDOMTR   Short-term domestic training.
       Yes = 55(30); No = 58(44)

35. OTHEROCC Have you had long-term employment (longer than one year) outside ORD?
    Yes = 10(4); No = 83(59)

36. HOMETOWN Where did you spend your childhood?
    Seoul = 15(15); Other city = 26(19);
    Rural area = 75(40)

37. DADJOB What is your father's occupation?
    Farmer = 56(31); Teacher = 8(6);
    Government = 10(9); Business = 16(12);
    Other = 5(5)

APPENDIX 6-B: KEY INFORMANT INTERVIEWS

Research Station Directors and Research Supervisors

The interviews with directors of the central and provincial research stations and heads of research sections focused on descriptions of the authority relationships within the agrobureaucracy and the types of extraorganizational influences that affected their research programs. This information was elicited by asking questions about specific organizational events and about how these were managed by the parties involved.

There is no substitute for location-specific knowledge about past events in this type of open-ended interviewing process. Especially when sensitive political questions were involved, questioning people about specific events in their daily work lives is easier than pursuing more abstract questions about the constraints of the political and bureaucratic systems under which they work. So, before interviewing in a particular provincial research station or central research institute, it was important to gain as much knowledge as possible about the provincial commodity production situation, past research system responses, and anticipated future problems. Interviews must build on past interviewing experiences. One incorporates much location-specific knowledge in this manner. Questions are continually being modified to reflect this new information. Generally, one finds that the interviews get better as the interviewing project moves along. In the course of such interviews, other prospective interviewees are often mentioned by respondents. Following up these leads proved quite beneficial. Also, in the course of reviewing past ORD research projects, it was possible to spot individuals who might have location-specific knowledge in important areas. These individuals were often added to the interview schedule in "snowball" fashion.

During the course of interviews with PORD and CORD directors and research section chiefs, the following issues were emphasized:

A. Personnel resources and management:
1. Discretionary powers of administrators over the budget, personnel allocations, and program direction;
2. Work histories of interviewees;
3. Assignment of research responsibilities to individual scientists;

4. Educational background and training opportunities for research scientists;
   5. Ranking system and promotion opportunities;
   6. Personnel evaluation procedures.
 B. Research program details:
   1. PORD-CORD division of labor;
   2. Division of labor within the institute;
   3. Commodity emphasis;
   4. Methods of setting research priorities;
   5. Research evaluation methods;
   6. Sources of demands placed on the research system;
   7. Research system response capacity.
 C. Problems and prospects for ORD research contributions.

Knowledgeable Outsiders

Within the Korean agricultural research community, it was quite useful to go outside the ORD organization to talk with individuals with close firsthand knowledge of ORD research projects. Most of these individuals had academic appointments at the time of the interview. Several had worked as ORD scientists in the past. Some had joint research appointments with ORD. Their "outsider" status may have encouraged a more objective perspective and/or allowed them more freedom to speak candidly about past ORD performance. The interview setting itself was often more congenial to a frank discussion of the issues. The interviews with ORD officials often had to proceed in the presence of others and were subject to interruptions. These "outsider" interviews served both as a reliability check and as a source of additional information.

Local Government Officials, Rural Guidance Officers, Farmers

In order to obtain more information about the ORD program at the local government and farm levels, interviews were conducted in South Kyongsang province for three weeks in July and August, 1982. The southern location was selected because of the agricultural diversity and high frequency of multiple cropping that characterize the region. A particular concern was to find out how the research system was responding to more complicated cropping system problems. Two counties were selected as interview sites. One was a traditional staple foodgrain production region with much upland cultivation.

It was geographically isolated and, hence, lacked the transportation infrastructure for cash crop marketing. The other county was located close to an urban area (Chinju) and major transportation arteries. Many farmers had shifted to a multiple-cropping regimen, often spring vegetables or melons followed by rice.

First interviewed were county administrators to see what agricultural development programs were emphasized at this jurisdictional level. Questions on local program autonomy, responses to provincial and national agricultural development programs, and farmer participation were emphasized. Eliciting location-specific information about ongoing government projects—for example, land rearrangement, the new village movement (*Saemaul Undong*), agricultural production campaigns, and programs to enhance farm income was an important goal. Information about the production and ecological characteristics of the township subunits within the county helped in the selection of regions for farmer and rural guidance officer interviews.

When interviewing rural guidance officers (RGOs) at the township level, location-specific questions were asked about the cropping systems in their jurisdictions, previous production problems and ORD responses, and RGO responsibilities. Emphasis was placed on finding out how RGOs related to farmers—the mode of farmer-RGO interaction, RGOs' perception of their mission, the backup support RGOs obtained from the research system at the PORD and CORD levels, and the ability (in terms of both educational training and bureaucratic flexibility) of RGOs to modify and adjust recommendations to fit local conditions. RGOs were asked to compare the Tongil and japonica rice varieties on the following traits: seedbed sowing time, transplanting time, yield potential, yield stability, labor requirements, fertilizer requirements, competitive ability against weeds, susceptibility to insects and disease, cold tolerance, drought resistance, compatability with double cropping, shattering, and taste characteristics. Questions about farmer marketing patterns and responses of the agrobureaucracy to specific production problems were also posed.

RGOs know all the farmers in their districts, so farmer contacts in a particular area were facilitated by initial contacts with responsible RGOs. Basic information was elicited from farmers about their farming operations—including cropping patterns, varietal selection, and marketing strategies. The same questions about Tongil and japonica adaptability were put to farmers to see if their observations matched those of the RGOs responsible for pushing government varietal recommendations. Farmers were asked to evaluate the RGOs' knowledge of particular agricultural problems. Other questions concerning the support received from the agrobureaucracy and the mode of interaction between farmers, the agrobureaucracy, and the local government were broached. A common method of interviewing in the Korean village context is to contact the village head (*rijang*). The *rijang* then introduces other farmers in the village. The "reputational" method of obtaining interviews tends to generate interviews with the the most well-connected, prosperous, innovative farmers in the village.

The in-depth, open-ended interviews at the farm and local government levels were means to corroborate information from published sources, the ORD research community, and others knowledgeable about the farmers' situation and farmers' reactions to the new technology (especially the Tongil rice varieties) developed and diffused by the ORD. Time and budget constraints limited the number of interviews obtained (a total of twenty-three interviews were transcribed—twelve with local government officials and rural guidance officers and eleven with farmers). Much information was gathered in informal settings when a structured interview schedule was not followed. No claims are made about the representativeness of these interviews. The interviews were quite useful, however, in giving the author a first-hand glimpse of the activities of the rural guidance officers and other local officials empowered to diffuse the new technologies developed by ORD. Farmers' responses to these interventions were also gleaned from these interviews and proved to be quite useful in interpreting how ORD products were being used.

7
Agricultural Research Policy in the NICs: Korea in Comparative Perspective

The preceding analysis of ORD activities illustrates how agricultural research decision making and program implementation are contingent on particular state/society relationships. If societal preferences are not articulated effectively in councils of state or in legislative arenas with meaningful allocative authority, it is unlikely that the provision of public goods, such as agricultural research, can be explained by adding up the weighted preferences of individuals or interest groups. Chapter 6 documented a lack of synergistic balance between administrative, scientific, and clientele pressures in agricultural research decision making in Korea. The interests of state agents rather than the interests of farmers, scientists, or consumers often determined priorities for agricultural research activities. The priorities of state agents were weighted toward alleviating emerging macroeconomic constraints to the nation's industrialization program.

Korea is not the only country where late industrialization coincided with BA (bureaucratic-authoritarian) politics. During the 1970s, the "elective affinity" between NIC successes (especially in Brazil, Taiwan, and Korea) and exclusionary BA political regimes received increasing attention in the literature on the political economy of third world development. While the role of agriculture in development has not assumed a high profile in the BA debate about the structural connection between latecomer industrialization and political exclusion of nonelite groups from public sector decision making, solutions to the "agrarian problem" loom large in all NIC industrialization efforts (except, of course, in the case of the NIC city-states,

Singapore and Hong Kong).

The "agrarian problem" refers to the need to extract surpluses from the agricultural sector in ways that provide economic support for industrialization. Owen (1966) used the phrase "double development squeeze" to describe effective modes of surplus extraction. Increased aggregate production must be induced on the farm, while, simultaneously, a flow of employable labor must be released from the countryside to industry. In the United States, for example, the "agricultural treadmill"—a combination of increased productivity, declining real commodity prices, and marginalization of small farm enterprises—provided the cheap wage goods and steady labor flows necessary to fuel the industrialization process. Public sector agricultural research was a key ingredient in the "treadmill" policy. In Korea, surplus labor was extracted from rural areas while significant productivity increases were coaxed from those remaining on the minifarms. The new rice production technology discussed in Chapter 4 played an important role in generating agricultural productivity advances.

The issue we address in this chapter is whether agricultural research policies in other NICs, especially those with similar BA political arrangements, resemble those found in Korea. Specifically, do the state/society relationships in other NICs foster similar patterns of state control over the agricultural research decision-making process? Furthermore, what impact have agricultural research decisions in these countries had on agrarian transformation outcomes? Hypothesized similarities in state/society relationships in Korea and other NICs justify brief comparisons. Both the BA literature (Collier 1979; Im 1987) and the dependent development literature (Evans 1979; Lim 1985) explicitly propose systematic comparative studies of Korea and other NICs (semiperipheral countries). The focus on agricultural research policymaking in this chapter brings us back to debates in development theory about the political economy of the agricultural research process outlined in Chapter 2. Comparisons will be made between Korea, Taiwan, and several Latin American NICs. The goal is to put what has been learned from the Korean experience into cross-national perspective in order to encourage further analysis of agricultural research policies as integral components of national development projects, conditioned by variations in two interdependent social structural axes—"internal" state/society relationships and "external" world system constraints and opportunities.

The Taiwanese Comparison

One strategy of historical-comparative inquiry stresses the selection of cases which are as alike as possible on all relevant analytical dimensions. The political economies of Korea and Taiwan converge in many important ways. Colonial domination by the same imperial power; a "labor surplus" monsoon rice economy (Oshima 1986); a unimodal agrarian structure (Johnston and Kilby 1975); endemic interstate conflict and subsequent societal militarization; and their incorporation into a regional political economy based on export industrialization (Cumings 1984a) are socioeconomic features common to both countries. Cumings (1984a) has coined the appellation "bureaucratic-authoritarian industrializing regime" (BAIR) to describe the political economies of Korea and Taiwan. This categorization implies, of course, that state/society relationships in the two countries are similar. By extrapolation, agricultural research decision-making structures, program trajectories, and program outcomes should be similar.

A review of the literature points to an important difference between the Korean and Taiwanese economic development experiences (see Scitovsky 1985:231-233; Kuo, Ranis, and Fei 1981). In Taiwan, more resources were extracted from agriculture to support the national industrialization project. There are several reasons for Taiwan's success in mobilizing a larger proportion of economic support for industrialization from its agricultural sector. Ecological differences have played an important role. Taiwan is blessed with a more robust agricultural climate. Semitropical conditions have provided both a wider range of commodity production choices and multiple cropping opportunities which are not available in Korea. Domestic staple food requirements for an increasing population were generated through productivity advances and cropping intensification (e.g., rice double cropping). In addition, tropical export commodities such as sugar generated a substantial amount of foreign exchange for the importation of capital goods required for industrialization. Despite respectable agricultural productivity gains, Korea achieved neither domestic food self-sufficiency nor generated substantial foreign exchange from agricultural exports. In addition to the ecological advantage, Taiwan, of course, did not suffer wartime infrastructure devastation comparable to that experienced on the Korean peninsula during the Korean War.

But social structural differences may also have played a role in Taiwan's more robust agricultural-industrialization linkage response. There seem to be no analogues in Taiwan to the Tongil green revolution campaign in Korea that we described in Chapter 4. Clough (1978) cites the "flexible" agricultural production system that combined government support with individual producer incentives as the key to agriculture's substantial contribution to industrialization in Taiwan. He concludes: "These dramatic results were made possible by a system that combined government action to provide needed market information, credit, and technical advice to both growers and processors with the freedom by farmers to make individual decisions as to what to grow" (Clough 1978:74). This may be an overly generous description of the relationship between state and countryside in Taiwan. For two decades, state officials established unfavorable terms of trade for agriculture through a rice-fertilizer barter system to extract more of the agricultural surplus for industrialization. Yet state agents at the local level were seemingly flexible in the promotion of new agricultural technologies. National production programs were apparently implemented in a more user-responsive administrative climate than existed in Korea. Although for many purposes it may be useful to group Korea and Taiwan together as BAIRs, there were important differences in state/society relationships that were manifested in variations in public sector agricultural research and extension responses in the countryside.

Key social structural features in Taiwan were the Joint Committee on Rural Reconstruction (JCRR) at the national level and farmers' associations (FAs) at the local level. The JCRR was a unique institutional outgrowth of U.S. economic assistance to China. This commission was established in 1948 before Chiang Kai-shek's flight from the mainland. The initiative was one among a number of midnight-hour attempts by the U.S. government to shore up nationalist fortunes in the Chinese Civil War. The commission was to serve an ombudsman function overseeing the disposition of U.S. economic assistance to make sure that fundamental agrarian reforms were being implemented in the countryside. When Chiang fled the mainland in 1949, the JCRR was retained to reassure the U.S. about the future allocation of much-needed financial assistance to facilitate a "new deal" for agriculture on Taiwan. Chiang finally realized that agrarian reform was necessary for the Kuomintang (KMT) refugee ruling elite to remain in power. The JCRR, composed of three Chinese and two American members, became the de facto Taiwanese ministry of agriculture in addition to its function as the agricultural command post for the large USAID mission on the island. Somewhat removed from KMT politics, this organizational apparatus provided a useful buffer between the state and the countryside, perhaps mitigating some of the overzealous mobilization impulses of a strong state bureaucracy.

The FAs were direct descendents of similar organizations formed during the Japanese colonial administration to diffuse improved agricultural technology, to encourage infrastructural (e.g., irrigation) development, and to provide credit and marketing channels. The primary purpose, of course, was to facilitate the flow of agricultural commodities to the Japanese homeland. The democratic aspects of the postcolonial FAs have perhaps been overemphasized in discussions of the accomplishments of Taiwanese agriculture (Apthorpe 1979; Moore 1984). Farmers were required to join FAs to be eligible for state-provided agricultural inputs and services—fertilizer being the most important commodity. The FAs, through the rice-fertilizer barter scheme and the nationalization of rice and sugar marketing, became the institutional vehicle through which the state replaced the expropriated landlord class as the appropriators of the agricultural surplus. On the other hand, some FA officials were elected from among the farmer clientele assuring a degree of informational feedback and responsiveness that the local government bureaucracy in Korea did not provide. Both research stations and extension operations were managed to some degree by the FAs, giving farmers more opportunity to voice preferences about the directions of technical change.

Cumings (1984b:11-12) suggests that important differential responses to colonial rule in Taiwan and Korea were due in large part to differences in agrarian social structures in the colonies. The agrarian structure in Taiwan approximated that in Japan, with a particularly important parallel being the emergence of "entrepreneurial landlords" who benefitted from colonial development programs. The agrarian landscape in Korea, on the other hand, was populated by a more recalcitrant, centuries-old aristocracy whose interests were not served by colonial development policies. In general, Taiwan was a much less troublesome colony for Japanese administrators. Civil administrators replaced military officials in top colonial administrative positions early on in Taiwan, whereas in Korea the amount of social turmoil caused by colonial rule required a military regime throughout the colonial interregnum.

The differential impact of colonial agricultural policies on rural living standards in Taiwan and Korea undoubtably colored peasants' perceptions of the effectiveness and benefits of state-sponsored R & E initiatives effected through the FAs in Taiwan and their agrobureaucratic analogues (i.e., local government administrative units) in Korea. Amsden (1979:348) declares that "the welfare of the Taiwanese peasant in the first half of the twentieth century may have exceeded that of the Japanese peasant—according to such welfare indices as type of wearing apparel, housing, local bank deposits, and the like." This situation contrasts starkly with absolute declines in rural living standards in colonial Korea (see Chapter 3). Thus a legacy of increased net income from official rural development efforts in Taiwan may have predisposed both the clientele and the agrobureaucracy to engage in more forthcoming cooperative patterns of behavior than characterized interaction between Korean peasants and government officials.

The success of Taiwanese R & E activities is manifested in the diversification of Taiwanese agriculture to meet changing internal and external demands. During the 1950s and 1960s, improved varieties of the major staple foodgrain, rice, and the prime export commodity, sugar, were developed and diffused throughout the island. The flexibility of the R & E system is reflected in the subsequent promotion of new crops and new farming techniques catering to new markets. Taiwanese agriculturalists appear to have shifted their commodity portfolios with alacrity, as evidenced by the increasing production of such high value crops as asparagus and mushrooms (primarily for export). According to official government statistics, the percentage of total agricultural production value attributable to high value specialty crops increased from 21.5% in 1952 to 60.5% in 1979; concurrently the share of rice in total production value fell from 50.2% to 26.8% (Kuo, Ranis, and Fei 1981:57). The activities of the FAs, and their ancillary R & E services, were apparently instrumental in facilitating farmer adaptation to changing economic conditions.

As in Korea, state officials in Taiwan created a pliable unimodal agrarian structure amenable to state control. In both countries, thorough land reforms did not lead to political empowerment in the countryside. If fact, the means of "political sanitation" in Taiwan were even more draconian than political control measures implemented in Korea. In 1947 the

KMT overlords in Taiwan began to liquidate systematically the native Taiwanese elite in response to "mass rebellion" against perceived KMT misrule on the island (Gold 1986; Amsden 1979). The culmination of this purge was the infamous "2-28 Incident" early in 1948 in which many Taiwanese were killed (Kerr 1965:30). This episode instilled in the Taiwanese the belief that "politics is dangerous" (Gold 1986:52). The stage was then set for subsequent KMT martial law administration on the island after the fall of Chiang on the mainland.

The "2-28 Incident" obviously heightened the divisions between the mainlanders and the Taiwanese and did not bode well for KMT reconstruction efforts on Taiwan. An economically self-sustaining Republic of China on Taiwan depended on the productive behavior of Taiwanese entrepreneurs and peasants. Mainlander KMT cadres controlled the strategic heights of the state (the bureaucracy and military) from 1949 on. Economic assets (land and labor), however, remained largely in the hands of the native Taiwanese majority population. The KMT elite undoubtably perceived the need to give native Taiwanese some meaningful decision-making latitude over day-to-day production activities in order to create an economic climate conducive to reconstruction. Important social divisions on Taiwan—mainlander refugees ruling over a socially distinct Taiwanese majority—made rural reorganization (e.g., land reform) relatively painless for KMT cadres (who were not landowners) but also made KMT rule problematic. Thus, concessions had to be made in areas of local autonomy and self-rule in order to ensure a modicum of political and economic support from producers (see Moore 1984:60-61); in socially homogeneous Korea this flexibility was not apparent. Within the confines of the bureaucratic-authoritarian regime type, a more accommodating political and economic modus vivendi was worked out between the state and the countryside in Taiwan than in Korea. One result was a more responsive agricultural research and extension operation in Taiwan.

The Latin American Comparison

Bureaucratic-authoritarian (BA) political regimes in Latin America were superimposed on a highly stratified class system. The emergence of similar regime types in Taiwan and South Korea, by contrast, occurred amidst considerable domestic social upheaval and international conflict following Japan's defeat in

World War II. The shift in Latin America from inclusionary "populist politics" in the 1940s and 1950s to exclusionary, military-dominant, "bureaucratic-authoritarian" politics in the 1960s and 1970s resulted from tacit agreements between the military and civilian elites to control increasingly vocal and disruptive political demands from a restless working class, the urban "marginals," and the peasant sector during the course of the industrialization process (see Collier 1979; Malloy 1987). State autonomy in Latin American BA regimes was constrained by the entrenched civilian social elites—the landed oligarchy and a rising entrepreneurial class in industry, retail trade, and agriculture. To make matters more complicated for state officials, fractions of the landed and entrepreneurial classes had long-standing alliances with foreign capital. Although the BA era did introduce the state as an important social force in the capital accumulation process, state officials had to accommodate the preexisting power structure. Unlike postwar Taiwan and Korea, the playing field on which industrialization and the agrarian transformation was to take place was already crowded. State officials did not have opportunities to restructure the internal social relations of capital accumulation in fundamental ways, nor were they able to regulate the mode of foreign capital penetration to the degree that characterized East Asian NIC adaptations. In other words, state officials in Latin American BA polities did not possess social autonomy commensurate to that enjoyed by their East Asian counterparts. The increased state intervention mounted by BA regimes in Latin America was in part a "Bonapartist" intervention to resolve stalemated class conflict (see Marx's *18th Brumaire*)—in part, a "developmental" response to problems of capital accumulation in late industrializing societies with both domestic and international capital in much stronger positions to bargain with state agents over the scope and means of state economic intervention.

Starting in the 1960s, renewed attention was focused on problems of agricultural stagnation in Latin America. From the interwar years to the mid-1950s, state officials were preoccupied with import substitution industrialization (ISI). Agricultural development remained in the background, as state investments were channeled to the industrial sector. However, ISI eventually created increased demands for foreign exchange. Agroexports were needed to pay for increased intermediate industrial imports. In addition, backsliding in agriculture encouraged increasing dependence on imported food staples. The foreign exchange drain stimulated renewed demands for an "agricultural import substitution" thrust to revitalize domestic staple food production systems. The general policy response, according to Grindle (1986), was to promote "agricultural modernization" programs oriented to the large-scale, commercial farm sector. Technological improvement and product/input/infrastructure subsidization policies were targeted toward capital-intensive and market-oriented farm operations. From the 1960s on, real government expenditures for agricultural development have increased substantially across Latin America, with agricultural R & E an integral component of "agricultural modernization" strategies.

Increased state investment in agricultural credit, research and extension, infrastructure, and mechanization was allocated within a highly differentiated agrarian sector. During the earlier period of agrarian capitalism in Latin America (mid-1800s to 1930), a "modern" capitalist farm sector was grafted onto historical *encomienda* and hacienda patterns of social domination. Extremely inegalitarian landholding patterns were combined with the retention of precapitalist socioeconomic controls over subsistence-oriented peasants and landless laborers. The result was a *latifundio/minifundio* commodity production system, often tied to international markets. Further introduction of capital-intensive technologies and promotion of large-scale production strategies reinforced agrarian social differentiation. The resource-poor *minifundios* and landless laborers were marginalized to an even greater extent due to increased pressures to alienate traditional peasant cultivation rights on productive land and to assure supplies of low-cost labor for seasonal agricultural production activities.

Continent-wide generalizations about agricultural R & E activities must be circumspect in light of the variations in state/society relationships in Latin American countries. Exclusionary, military-controlled regimes came to power in Brazil, Argentina, Chile, Peru, and Uruguay (among others) from the 1950s to the early 1970s. In Mexico, civilian one-party rule continued with sporadic attempts to coopt those groups (primarily politically restless peasants) left behind by industrialization and agricultural development programs. Colombia and Venezuela managed to survive the BA phase with their competitive, civilian political systems intact. In spite of these variations, similarities in agrarian structure and in the way state interventions in the agricultural economy were designed to accommodate that structure make it possible to offer some generalizations about state/society relationships and agricultural research policies and programs which put the Latin American experience and our previous discussion of the East Asian experience in comparative perspective.

Recent studies of agricultural research activities in Latin America document "biases" in the technical and social outcomes (Sanders and Ruttan 1978; de Janvry 1981; Pineiro and Trigo 1983; de Janvry and Dethier 1985; Grindle 1986). Agricultural productivity advances have been uneven across commodities, regions, and countries (see Pineiro and Trigo 1983:38-39; Grindle 1986:82-83,88). Campaigns to increase staple food production for the domestic market have been directed toward introduced commodities such as wheat and rice, often as agricultural import substitution initiatives to provision the urban-industrial sector. Export commodities—soybeans, coffee, bananas, beef, industrial crops, etc.—have also received sustained attention. Indigenous domestic food staples such as maize and beans, which often are the mainstays of peasant subsistence-oriented agricultural production systems, have been neglected in national commodity improvement programs. Maize for the peasants' tortillas has received relatively little agricultural R & E attention; corn for the beef exporters' feedlots has received considerably more agricultural R & E support. The faultlines of commodity research intensity parallel the commercial farm and peasant farm agrarian divide. Agricultural research initiatives have been promulgated on a "socially selective" basis.

As mentioned in Chapter 2, de Janvry and Dethier (1985) outline the "class efficiency" dynamics of effective societal demand for agricultural research in many Latin American countries. In cases where agricultural research initiatives can be identified as responses to changing market signals, the bimodal agrarian power structure has created institutional forces that have "distorted" agricultural markets, sending off misleading relative price signals. For example, subsidies to capital encourage mechanization amidst a labor surplus in the countryside. Artificially cheap capital creates a latent demand for further capital-intensive, labor-saving technological improvements among the politically powerful large-scale, commercial farm operators. Historically, the accumulation of social and economic resources through differential access to prime land and secure supplies of water, organizational networks, and information channels places commercially-oriented farmers in the most advantageous positions to gain access to and to make productive use of state-proferred production subsidies, infrastructural improvements, and technical assistance. Targeting this responsive clientele makes the most sense to state agents whose goal is to maximize aggregrate production outputs from agricultural research investments.

"Class-efficient" tendencies in public sector agricultural research responses do not mean that there is no flexibility in the way that productivity-enhancing projects are identified and implemented. de Janvry and Dethier (1985), interpreting earlier case studies analyzed by Pineiro and Trigo (1983), note that different "paths of technological transformation" often occur within the same country. That is, there are occasions when the state acts "from above" to generate new technologies for a targeted commodity and group of producers; in other instances, state-funded agricultural R & E programs are activated "from below." These different modes of state/society response are conditioned primarily by variations in the structure of the agricultural sector—farm structure (operational size, commercial orientation, labor supply) and market structure (regional/national/international importance of commodities).

Paradoxically, this seeming flexibility in state/society response patterns has not produced agricultural R & E programs with noticeably robust economic development outcomes, if one views development more in terms of intersectoral linkage and sectoral incorporation rather than merely in terms of aggregate economic growth effects. de Janvry (1981), in particular, has analyzed the striking degree of "disarticulation" within Latin American economies. Within the agricultural sector, disarticulation means that growth has been unevenly distributed across commodities, regions, and farm types. Subsistence-oriented peasant producers and landless laborers, those groups in the agrarian economy most in need of additional sources of income through increased articulation with the national economy, have often been bypassed by improvements in agricultural technology and infrastructure. As a consequence, socioeconomic marginalization in the countryside has increased, fostering more problematic dependency relationships between the state, capitalist farmers, and an agrarian underclass. From a national development perspective, marginalization limits the robustness of intersectoral linkages, both on the demand and the supply sides. The entire national development project is threatened when entrenched sectoral dualism blocks the emergence of mass-based consumer goods and production input industries that draw the countryside into a national market economy.

From a comparative perspective, agricultural sector disarticulation does not appear to be a function of aggregate expenditures on agricultural research. Mexico, Venezuela, Brazil, Chile, Colombia, and Peru have invested more in agricultural research (as measured by agricultural research expenditures as a percentage of agricultural GDP) than Korea (see de Janvry and Dethier 1985:25). Yet in Korea, a lower level of agricultural research investment seems to have produced a more articulated economic response, at least during the past two decades. Substantial, across-the-board increases in rural household income and consumption have occurred (Kim and Joo 1982). Technological advances are partly responsible. How research is targeted to particular types of farm enterprises and the adequacy of the technical support system (e.g., provision of requisite production inputs), rather than relative levels of research expenditures, tend to determine the economic spread effects of agricultural development programs based on improved technologies. It is certainly the case that colonial interest in peasant food staples and an ecologically homogeneous production environment were important factors in promoting more articulated agricultural development outcomes in the East Asian NICs. Nevertheless, a major factor explaining the articulation/disarticulation difference is agrarian structure—the way rural power relationships and social resource bases affected the allocation and utilization of agricultural R & E resources. How the state as a "development agency" reacts to societal pressures depends on what kind of rural social landscape state officials must operate in.

State officials in the Latin American and East Asian NICs have quite similar goals for agriculture. State intervention in the agricultural economy is designed to set in motion the agrarian transformation. A reinvigorated agricultural sector promises to ease the macroeconomic constraints which often threaten the national industrialization project. In Latin America, agrarian dualism has increased greatly the difficulty state officials have in effecting an all-encompassing agrarian transformation that integrates most agricultural producers into intersectoral markets in a way that promotes "articulated" economic growth. This situation contrasts sharply with the East Asian experience wherein the agrarian transformation was managed "from above" by *simultaneously* restructuring production relations within the agricultural sector, promulgating "positive-sum" policy measures that induced increased production responses, and empowering an effective agrobureaucracy to diffuse new technology and extract a surplus. In the East Asian NICs, the unimodal agrarian structure facilitated the design of agricultural research strategies that targeted the vast majority of farmers. Attention was focused on commodities that were of paramount importance to the average individual farm household and the national economy. The conflicting goals of agrarian transformation—providing cheap wage goods for industry, the release of productive labor to industry, the supply of capital to industry (either through wage goods' import substitution [Taiwan and Korea] or agroexports [Taiwan]), and the creation of rural markets for industrial products (production inputs and consumer goods)—have been achieved to a greater extent in East Asian than in Latin American NICs. Not only has the rural sector been integrated into national markets for goods and services, but this incorporation has occurred in a way that raised living standards for the vast majority of the rural population.

Patterns of State Intervention and Societal Response

State officials in the NICs invariably intervene in agricultural production relations to speed up the agrarian transformation. State-sponsored agricultural research initiatives discussed in this and preceding chapters are prime examples. Are state officials and their organizations positioned to exert control over strategic agricultural production relations; are societal forces on the local and national scenes strong enough to sabotage state initiatives in ways that deflect development programs from their original intent; or is it possible to reconcile both state and societal preferences in ways that promote mutually satisfactory outcomes? It is argued below that Korea approaches the first scenario, many Latin American countries the second, and Taiwan the third. The following discussion follows to an extent Migdal's (1985) conceptualization of variation in state/society relations.

Both "liberal" and "radical" scholars agree that reformist agricultural development programs in Latin America designed to effect a simultaneous increase in aggregate productivity and a significant reduction in rural poverty have failed (see Grindle 1986; de Janvry 1981). The stark fact about the Latin American political economy is that formal independence did not restructure agrarian power relationships in any fundamental way. Even the Mexican Revolution, which was to a degree peasant-based (see Wolf 1969, Ch. 1), failed to overhaul the rural sector. The most sustained efforts to implement an enduring agrarian reform occurred during the Cardenas presidency (1934-1940) with land redistribution to *ejidal* communal holdings and to other small-scale peasant producers. However, plantations in semitropical regions, the opening of large tracts of irrigated land in the northwest and northcentral regions, and huge ranches in other semiarid northern regions combined to form a complex mix of landholding patterns, commodity orientations, and technologies of production in which agrarian political and economic power remained quite skewed, favoring large-scale commercial producers. Few Latin American countries have even approximated Mexico's attempt to reverse *latifundio/minifundio* dualism. The result is the continuing social domination of the "commercial *hacendado*" in the Latin American countryside.

In the Latin American rural context, the large-scale commercial producers control so many physical and organizational resources that they are often the only producer group that can make effective use of a range of state-proferred productive incentives and subsidies. Local monopoly control over land and labor transforms original agricultural development interventions, conceived as broad-based production stimuli, into subsidies for agrarian elites. This transformation emasculates state-sponsored attempts to reduce rural socioeconomic disarticulation. Even if state officials try to target the peasant sector, the paucity of complementary resources means that outreach programs have little impact and/or large-scale, commercialized interests will usurp the programs by encroaching further on peasants' rights over land and labor services.

In addition to constraints on state initiatives resulting from skewed distributions of resources within society, state administrators are not linked politically to the rural masses. Latin American political parties traditionally have been weak. When party organizations have emerged, they have been more likely to organize around urban-industrial and agroexport interests. Occasionally, as in the Mexican one-party polity, the peasant sector has generated enough political voice to force sporadic pushes for peasant empowerment (e.g., land redistribution). Mexico is the exception to the rule in Latin American politics, and redistributive programs there have not been successful to the extent that the majority of peasant farmers are effectively incorporated into more productive, intersectoral socioeconomic relationships. The BA political phase in Latin America, in particular, has emphasized de-politicization of socially restive urban and rural groups.

In Korea, local constraints on state activities during the 1960s and 1970s were extraordinarily weak. As emphasized earlier in Chapter 3, the minifarm structure of Korean agriculture has mitigated against the formation of an agrarian power bloc that can lobby effectively in informal, closed state/society bargaining arenas. Furthermore, grassroots political organizations in the countryside have been drastically curtailed. Rural organizational initiatives such as the *Saemaul Undong* have been created and manipulated from above. Both Presidents Park and Chun created "government" political parties from above, often using state machinery such as the Korean CIA. Opposition forces have mustered very little organizational machinery to compete with the government party apparatus. A rural social landscape populated by minifarms and devoid of effective countervailing political organization has given state officials a relatively free hand in fashioning agricultural development policy packages (see Chapter 4) that satisfy state preferences for broad-based agricultural sector incorporation into the national economy.

Taiwan presents a more balanced picture of state agricultural development initiatives designed to satisfy state preferences for robust agroindustrial linkages, combined with some mediating societal controls over program trajectories and implementation at the local level. The relative political weakness of the agricultural sector attributable to minifarm agriculture is somewhat buffered by the societal power of the native Taiwanese majority, a mundane demographic reality the ruling mainlander elite must continually cope with. The membership of the previously discussed FAs, for example, is primarily native Taiwanese. These organizations are involved in day-to-day bargaining with local government officials over the administration and implementation of state-supported agricultural development measures. In addition to the FA organizational presence, the KMT's cellular organizational structure has required the gradual assimilation of native Taiwanese cadres, at least at the local level, during the course of the KMT's four-decade-long rule. In contrast to Korea's ephemeral political party organizations, the KMT has a long history as a political organization separate from the Taiwanese state machinery. Through the KMT local branch organizations, rural societal interests can percolate up to higher party and state policy councils. While we are not able to delve deeply into the nature of the party-state fusion here, it is evident that KMT political organization in Taiwan is a separate social mobilization instrument that penetrates deeply into society. Nothing comparable exists in Latin America, with the possible exception of PRI (the revolutionary party) in Mexico. This degree of political articulation is also foreign to the Korean political scene, where political parties have tended to be ancillary, expedient administrative organs of the state subject to instant dissolution at the time of government reorganization by the executive or excecutive removal.

The preceding discussion illustrates the fact that significant variations in state/society relations coexist within political economies which are sometimes grouped together as BA regimes. These variations serve notice that a generic BA structure conditioned by semiperipheral location within the world system does not exist. The Northeast Asian BAIRs and the Latin American BA regimes emerged under quite different macrosocial contexts—colonial legacies, timing of independence and industrialization, types of external economic linkages, and geopolitical situations. Thus, state/society relations within the BA regimes are different; accordingly, agricultural research policy and agricultural development responses have varied. The cases do offer some important lessons about world system linkages and the crystallization of patterns of state/society relationships in third world settings.

From Agricultural Research Policy to World System Theory

From the mundane world of agricultural research policy, we move to the rarefied heights of world system theory. Koo's (1984) discussion of the relation between state, class, and world system summarizes succinctly the heuristic legacy of dependency theory and world system theory for comparative studies of third world societies. It is now difficult to ignore the fact that what happens in these societies is conditioned in a significant way by the structure and dynamics of the world system. We argue that the relationship between state, class, and world system can be more fully understood if we move away from economically reductionist conceptualizations of world system structure toward more multivalent schemas in order to get a complete picture of how "politics works from the outside in" (see Giddens 1985, Ch. 7). In particular, the interstate-geopolitical and the capitalist-economic dimensions of the modern world system must be recognized as having separate, even if often interconnected, influences on the emergence of state/society relations in the third world.

The aforementioned warfare/welfare developmental imperative thrust upon ruling elites in the new nations has necessitated "associative" strategies (see Ruggie 1983c) of world system engagement—that is, the forging of military and/or economic ties with first world advanced capitalist and/or second world state socialist camps in order to obtain scarce resources which are not available internally. The structural impact on internal state/society relationships depends on when and under what conditions these exchanges are consummated. Eberhard's (1968) notion of "world time" is relevant here. Structural parameters of the modern world system change. Politically, the uneasy multipolar balance of power of the competitive pre-World War I European interstate system (plus the United States and Japan) was succeeded by a bipolar world with liberal capitalist and state socialist spheres of influence. Economically, the hegemony of British "free trade liberalism" and global commercial expansion was succeeded by a U.S.-designed "embedded liberal" regime (Ruggie 1983a) during which global TNC expansion was encouraged in tandem with the increased economic intervention of the welfare state. The impact of the timing of associative engagement for the power positions of state officials and societal forces in East Asian and Latin American NICs will be discussed below.

In the Latin American NICs, state officials have not gained social domination over the domestic capitalist class, nor has the state been able to dictate the terms of multinational capital entry to the extent seen in East Asia. The BA political economy phase in Latin America did not produce state hegemony. This relative weakness of the Latin American state must be traced back to early postindependence alliances between the landed oligarchy and British commercial interests, which encouraged laissez-faire state/society arrangements. The social power of the landed elites within Latin American societies was solidified further, fostering a mode of social domination that exists in modified form (landed elite-industrial alliance) today. Continuing economic ties to the advanced capitalist world often took the form of U.S. direct investment in Latin American agroexport and industrial activities. The ongoing alliance between domestic and foreign capital was further cemented by post-World War II TNC penetration.

During the nineteenth century, the U.S. began to expand its geopolitical sphere of influence, first by enunciating the Monroe Doctrine. As a result, serious incursions into Latin American domestic politiomilitary and economic affairs began in the midnineteenth century and have continued to the present. Until the outbreak of the Cold War, the U.S. was content with a circulation of ruling elites—basically factions of the landed oligarchy—so long as commercial projects of U.S. nationals and firms were not threatened. Military force was used occasionally to depose a ruling clique if debts were reneged upon or if an important commercial project was stymied by internal politics (e.g., the Panama Canal). Concern about the internal structure of Latin American state apparatuses grew following the outbreak of the Cold War and especially with the culmination of the successful socialist revolution in Cuba. Internal revolutionary threats from below became the impetus for U.S. foreign assistance to shore up the internal state structure, particularly the military. The end result was a flow of military assistance to Latin American countries in the form of hardware and organizational training. Consequently, the military as an organization gained in corporate strength vis-à-vis other state officials and societal actors (Horowitz 1982). A revitalized military combined the mission of "societal pacification" with a novel commitment to economic development, altering the internal social landscape in many Latin American countries.

BA regimes in Latin America were fashioned in this international context. Social ties between the strengthened military and the old civilian ruling elites remained strong. Mass conscription has not occurred to the degree that facilitates access of all social strata to high-ranking military positions. Evans' (1979) "tri-pe" alliance of state, domestic capital, and international capital bargained over their respective economic niches and functions in the national industrial project. This alliance did not countenance strong reformist initiatives, such as significant redistributions of economic assets. As was explored earlier, the agricultural policy result was an "agricultural modernization" strategy targeted toward the large-scale, commercial sector. Agrarian dualism and socioeconomic disarticulation deepened. Reinvigorated agricultural research initiatives were socially biased. As Grindle (1986) argues, the autonomous decision-making capacity of the state did increase during the postwar period. But state officials were constrained in important ways by entrenched class actors who could not be excised from the social landscape without jeopardizing the existing pact of social domination. In Peru, in particular, peasant empowerment projects implemented by state officials were curtailed because they threatened to unleash social forces which could not be controlled. Grindle (1986:4-5) concludes:

> The range of options available to state elites was constrained by the growth of the economic and political power of large-scale capitalist entrepreneurs; radical changes in the structure of agricultural production and capitalist accumulation were thus ruled out as economically and politically infeasible. Instead, a variety of policies were introduced to manage or compensate for the problems of poverty, underproductivity, and international dependence that capitalist expansion had brought in its wake. This stimulated further state penetration of the rural economy and social structures. Thus, over time, the state increased its capacity to address and manage protests of the rural poor arising from conflict over land and livelihood.

In summary, world system intrusions on local state/society relationships in the postindependence period fostered the emergence of a socially dominant, landed oligarchy-commercial elite, first through through the expansion of primary commodity trade and later through the expansion of TNC enterprises. The state apparatus was strengthened as a consequence of ISI industrialization pushes and external military assistance, but it remained "class-oriented." The present "redemocratization" of Latin American politics does not presently pose a threat to this arrangement (see Malloy 1987).

The contrast between East Asian and Latin American world system articulation patterns is striking. Formal independence in Korea and the KMT retreat to Taiwan occurred amidst growing postwar superpower geopolitical conflict. Worldwide militarization and the formation of bipolar political economies quickly followed in the wake of the formation of NATO, the Bretton Woods financial institutions, the Warsaw Pact, and COMECON. The most fortunate new nations could use the superpower split as a developmental bargaining chip. Those less fortunately positioned were quickly sucked into the Cold War. Korea and Taiwan, located at geopolitical flashpoints, were archetypes of the latter situation. Autonomous decision-making capacities of state officials in Taiwan and Korea were constantly recharged by the social reservoir of state power embedded in their precarious geopolitical situations. Civilian social actors were from the start definitely junior partners in subsequent development initiatives.

Vast amounts of resources were channeled into the Taiwanese and Korean military establishments. KMT control in Taiwan meant an early fusion of military and bureaucratic cadres at the commanding heights of the state apparatus. The KMT withdrawal to Taiwan was a military operation; Taiwan has been on martial law footing until this year. Societal mobilization was justified first as a defensive measure against imminent attack from the mainland. Later on, economic development in the service of continual confrontation with the People's Republic became a prime goal requiring ubiquitous state intervention in the economic life of the island. The end result was the formation of industrial enterprises and parastatal infrastructural support systems under the direct management of the state bureaucracy. Private entrepreneurs took a backseat to the public enterprise sector for three decades. Even now, state-owned corporations still number among the largest economic entities on the island. The relatively favorable agricultural environment in Taiwan coupled with a corps of trained public officials who fled from the mainland provided a favorable resource base for state-directed, force-fed industrialization.

In Korea, the militarization of society was a consequence of the Korean War. Universal conscription was retained as a defense measure following the cessation of hostilities, with important social structural implications. The post-Korean War Rhee regime was a disappointment both in terms of economic and political development. Only the military survived the social confusion of the last Rhee years as a powerful corporate social group capable of taking control of the state apparatus. The military proved to be an avenue of social mobility for youth from modest social backgrounds. Thus, the military coup in 1961 brought into power a social group with weak ties to elites in government and business. This social distance provided the military junta with opportunities to rearrange social power relationships. In the end, both civilian bureaucratic elites and the incipient entrepreneurial class were conscripted to carry out the state-directed economic development mandates as junior partners under the watchful eyes of former military personnel who now controlled the executive branch and its watchdog agencies. This arrangement consolidated capacity for autonomous policymaking actions by state agents.

Both Taiwan and Korea were frontline U.S. client states in the Cold War. Kihl (1984:155) estimates that Korea received a total of U.S. $12.6 billion from 1946 through 1975, approximately half of which was military assistance. Without such assistance, the Rhee regime would not have survived. The longevity of the increasingly repressive Park regime would also have been in jeopardy without rapid economic growth which compensated for, at least for a time, public disappointment over the lack of political liberalization. Easy access to world markets at a time of unparalleled international economic expansion and financial benefits from "invited" Korean participation in the Vietnam War were benefits provided by "client state" status without which the Korean "development miracle" would certainly have been much more problematic. Similar politicoeconomic arrangements bound Taiwan to U.S. apron strings. This dependency profile has led radical scholars and internal dissidents to challenge the nationalist credentials of current and past ruling elites in both Korea and Taiwan.

Somewhat paradoxically, however, this external relationship has engendered a state/society relationship at variance, in fundamental political and economic ways, with American preferences for a "liberal capitalist" social order. The American postwar plan for world order was characterized by its relative openness. According to Cumings (1984a:6-7):

> In the postwar American case, hegemony meant the demarcation a "grand area." Within that area nations oriented themselves toward Washington rather than Moscow; nations were enmeshed in a hierarchy of economic and political preferences whose ideal goal was free trade, open systems, and

liberal democracy but which also encompassed neomercantile states and authoritarian politics; and nations were dealt with by the United States through methods ranging from classic negotiations and trade-offs (in regard to nations sharing Western traditions or approximating American levels of political and economic development) to wars and interventions (in the periphery or Third World), to assure continuing orientation toward Washington. The hegemonic ideology, shared by most Americans but by few in the rest of the world, was the Tocquevillean or Hartzian ethos of liberalism and internationalism, assuming a born-free country that never knew class conflict. Not a colonial or neocolonial imperialism, it was a new system of empire begun with Wilson and consummated by Roosevelt and Acheson. Its very breadth—its nonterritoriality, its universalism, and its open systems (within the grand area)—made for a style of hegemony that was more open than previous imperialisms to competition from below. Indeed, we may eventually conclude that this was its undoing.

Krasner (1985:72-75) notes the emphasis on the principle of "sovereign equality of states" that has guided U.S. ideas about dominant world order since Wilson's call for national self-determination in the colonial territories. This world view has made it difficult for U.S. policymakers to control the internal political economies of so-called client states in ways that mesh with U.S. ideals of federalism, multiple social sources of policy initiatives, firm commitment to private sector rather than statist economic initiatives, and civilian control of the military. In particular, social groups within Korea and Taiwan (namely the military and the state bureaucracy) seized external resources to build internal social power bases. Attempts by U.S. policymakers, direct and indirect, to refashion the state/society relationships in such allied third world countries along "bourgeoisie democratic" lines have not been successful.

A case exemplifying the way U.S. assistance has been used to generate antithetical social organizational outcomes is the institutionalization of ORD in Korea. As mentioned earlier, the U.S. provided considerable financial and technical assistance to develop institutionalized agricultural research and extension capacity in Korea. Korean state officials used this assistance to create an agricultural R & E system which was based on quite different sociopolitical assumptions about how agricultural research intiatives should be decided upon and diffused. In effect, U.S. financial and technical resources were coopted to strengthen an agrobureaucracy organized along bureaucratic centralist, rather than decentralized pluralist, lines. Organizationally, ORD resembled the Japanese colonial agrobureaucratic apparatus more than the U.S. land-grant agricultural research and extension system.

In both Korea and Taiwan, the geopolitical world system pressures in the immediate postwar era created a military-dominated state apparatus with formidable autonomy vis-à-vis societal interests. Only recently have private sector interests achieved enough countervailing power to challenge state hegemony in important national policymaking arenas. Developmental initiatives under state leadership have created civilian social classes based on the division of labor in industrial society in Taiwan and Korea. Now, it is no longer possible to ignore the demands of big business and the middle classes for political and economic liberalization. A new relationship between the state and these emerging social classes is now the focal point of political liberalization drives in both countries. An accommodation will not come easily. However, a peaceful denouement is likely to require a "corporate" solution, meaning that state officials will be directly involved in determining how societal interests will be organized to facilitate orderly bargaining over public policy. Agricultural research policymaking, especially in Korea, may become more responsive to societal forces if this change is effected. However, it is likely that the state will remain quite active in restructuring the agricultural sector to facilitate socioeconomic adjustment to continuing industrialization.

The realpolitik objective of competitive industrialization within the modern world system continues to drive neo-merchantilist industrial policy in both Korea and Taiwan. But both internal social structural changes and the current depth of the external economic engagement have altered the ability of state officials to unilaterally establish the scope and mode of state economic intervention. Key policy issues—foreign capital penetration, industrial organization, capital/labor relations, etc.—will be determined increasingly in more "pluralistic" national and international decision-making arenas. The state apparatus is still strong, but ongoing articulation between the state, society, and the ever-changing world system has fostered countervailing power centers that control enough resources to force bargaining accommodations.

References

Adelman, Irma, and Sherman Robinson. 1978. *Income Distribution in Developing Countries: A Case Study of Korea.* Stanford, CA: Stanford University Press.

Alavi, Hamza. 1972. "The State in Post-Colonial Societies: Pakistan and Bangladesh." *New Left Review* 74:59-81.

Aldrich, Howard. 1979. *Organizations and Environments.* Englewood Cliffs, NJ: Prentice-Hall, Inc.

Amsden, Alice. 1979. "Taiwan's Economic History: A Case of Etatisme and a Challenge to Dependency Theory." *Modern China* 5:341-380.

Anderson, Kym. 1983. "Growth of Agricultural Protection in East Asia." *Food Policy* 8:327-336.

Apthorpe, Raymond. 1979. "The Burden of Land Reform in Taiwan: An Asian Model Land Reform Re-Analyzed." *World Development* 7:519-530.

Aqua, Ronald. 1974. *Local Institutions and Rural Development in South Korea.* Ithaca, NY: Cornell University, Rural Development Committee, Center for International Studies.

Bacharach, Samuel, and Edward J. Lawler. 1980. *Power and Politics in Organizations.* San Francisco: Jossey-Bass Publishers.

Ban, Sung Hwan. 1985. "A Review on the Policies and Sources for Economic and Agricultural Development in Korea." *Agricultural Research of Seoul National University* 10:95-110.

Ban, Sung Hwan, Pal Yong Moon, and Dwight H. Perkins. 1980. *Rural Development.* Cambridge, MA: Harvard University Press.

Bank of Korea. 1962-1986. *Bank of Korea Statistical Yearbooks.* Seoul: Bank of Korea.

Barker, Randolph, and Robert W. Herdt with Beth Rose. 1985. *The Rice Economy of Asia.* Washington, DC: Resources for the Future, Inc.

Barone, Charles A. 1983. "Dependency, Marxist Theory, and Salvaging the Idea of Capitalism in Korea." *Review of Radical Political Economics* 15:43-67.

Bell, Daniel. 1973. *The Coming Post-Industrial Society.* New York: Basic Books, Inc.

Bendix, Reinhard. 1967. "Tradition and Modernity Reconsidered." *Comparative Studies in Society and History* 9:292-346.

Berry, R. A. 1975. "Special Problems in Policy Making in

Technologically Heterogeneous Agriculture: Colombia." Pp. 253-296 in *Agriculture in Development Theory*, edited by Lloyd G. Reynolds. New Haven, CT: Yale University Press.
Binswanger, Hans P., Vernon W. Ruttan, and others. 1978. *Induced Innovation: Technology, Institutions, and Development*. Baltimore: The Johns Hopkins University Press.
Boyce, James K., and Robert E. Evenson. 1975. *National and International Agricultural Research and Extension Programs*. New York: Agricultural Development Council, Inc.
Brandt, Vincent S. R., and Man-Gap Lee. 1981. "Community Development in the Republic of Korea." Pp. 49-136 in *Community Development: Comparative Case Studies in India, the Republic of Korea, Mexico and Tanzania*, edited by Ronald Dore and Zoe Mars. London: Croon Helm.
Browett, John. 1985. "The Newly Industrializing Countries and Radical Theories of Development." *World Development* 13: 789-803.
Burmeister, Larry L. 1985. State, Society, and Agricultural Research Policy: The Case of South Korea. Unpublished Ph.D. dissertation, Cornell University.
_____. 1986. "Warfare, Welfare, and State Autonomy: Structural Roots of the South Korean Developmental State." *Pacific Focus* 1:121-146.
_____. 1987a. "The South Korean Green Revolution: Induced or Directed Innovation?" *Economic Development and Cultural Change* 35:766-790.
_____. 1987b. State, Industrialization, and Agricultural Policy in Korea. Unpublished manuscript.
_____. 1987c. "Social Domination in Korean Society: A Neoweberian Interpretation." Paper presented at the 39th annual meeting of the Association for Asian Studies, Boston.
Busch, Lawrence, and William B. Lacy. 1983. *Science, Agriculture, and the Politics of Research*. Boulder, CO: Westview Press.
Busch, Lawrence, William B. Lacy, and Carolyn Sachs. 1980. Research Policy and Process in the Agricultural Sciences: Some Results from a National Study. Lexington: Agricultural Experiment Station, College of Agriculture, Department of Sociology, University of Kentucky.
Buzan, Barry. 1983. *People, States, and Fear: The National Security Problem in International Relations*. Chapel Hill:

The University of North Carolina Press.
Cardoso, Fernando Henrique, and Enzo Faletto. 1979. *Dependency and Development in Latin America*. Berkeley: University of California Press.
Carnoy, Martin. 1984. *The State and Political Theory*. Princeton, NJ: Princeton University Press.
Chalmers, Douglas A. 1985. "Corporatism and Comparative Politics." Pp. 56-79 in *New Directions in Comparative Politics*, edited by Howard J. Wiarda. Boulder, CO: Westview Press.
Chen, Ching-chih. 1984. "Police and Community Control Systems in the Empire." Pp. 213-239 in *The Japanese Colonial Empire, 1895-1945*, edited by Ramon H. Myers and Mark R. Peattie. Princeton, NJ: Princeton University Press.
Cho, Chang Hyun. 1972. "Bureaucracy and Local Government in South Korea." Pp. 91-126 in *Government and Politics in Korea*, edited by Se-Jin Kim and Chang Hyun Cho. Silver Spring, MD: The Research Institute on Korean Affairs.
Clough, Ralph N. 1978. *Island China*. Cambridge, MA: Harvard University Press.
Cole, David C., and Princeton N. Lyman. 1971. *Korean Development: The Interplay of Politics and Economics*. Cambridge, MA: Harvard University Press.
Cole, David C., and Yung Chul Park. 1983. *Financial Development in Korea, 1945-1978*. Cambridge, MA: Harvard University Press.
Cole, Jonathan R., and Stephen Cole. 1973. *Social Stratification in Science*. Chicago: The University of Chicago Press.
Collier, David, ed. 1979. *The New Authoritarianism in Latin America*. Princeton, NJ: Princeton University Press.
Collins, Randall. 1968. "A Comparative Approach to Political Sociology." Pp. 42-69 in *State and Society*, edited by Reinhard Bendix, et al. Berkeley: University of California Press.
_____. 1986. *Weberian Sociological Theory*. Cambridge: Cambridge University Press.
Crane, Diana. 1972. *Invisible Colleges*. Chicago: The University of Chicago Press.
Crill, Pat, Y. S. Ham, and H. M. Beachell. 1982. *The Rice Blast Disease and its Control with Race Prediction and Gene Rotation*. Los Banos, Philippines: International Rice Research Institute.

Cumings, Bruce. 1981. *The Origins of the Korean War.* Princeton, NJ: Princeton University Press.

―――, ed. 1983. *Child of Conflict: The Korean-American Relationship, 1943-1953.* Seattle: University of Washington Press.

―――. 1984a. "The Origins and Development of the Northeast Asian Political Economy: Industrial Sectors, Product Cycles, and Political Consequences." *International Organization* 38:1-40.

―――. 1984b. "The Legacy of Japanese Colonialism in Korea." Pp. 479-496 in *The Japanese Colonial Empire, 1895-1945*, edited by Ramon H. Myers and Mark R. Peattie. Princeton, NJ: Princeton University Press.

Dahl, Robert A., and Charles E. Lindblom. 1953. *Politics, Economics, and Welfare.* Chicago: The University of Chicago Press.

Dalrymple, Dana G. 1980. *Development and Spread of HYVs of Wheat and Rice in Less Developed Countries.* Washington, DC: United States Department of Agriculture.

―――. 1985. Development of High-Yielding Rice Varieties in the Developing Countries. CGIAR Staff Paper. Washington, DC: USAID, Bureau for Science and Technology.

―――. 1986. *Development and Spread of High-Yielding Rice Varieties in Developing Countries.* Washington, DC: USAID, Bureau for Science and Technology.

Danbom, Charles. 1979. *The Resisted Revolution.* Ames: The Iowa State University Press.

de Janvry, Alain. 1978. "Social Structure and Biased Technical Change in Argentine Agriculture." Pp. 297-323 in *Induced Innovation*, edited by Hans P. Binswanger and Vernon W. Ruttan. Baltimore: The Johns Hopkins University Press.

―――. 1981. *The Agrarian Question and Reformism in Latin America.* Baltimore: The Johns Hopkins University Press.

―――. 1984. "The Role of Land Reform in Economic Development: Policies and Politics." Pp. 263-274 in *Agricultural Development in the Third World*, edited by Carl K. Eicher and John M. Staatz. Baltimore: The Johns Hopkins University Press.

de Janvry, Alain, and Jean Jacques Dethier. 1985. *Technological Innovation in Agriculture: The Political Economy of its Rate and Bias.* CGIAR Staff Paper No. 1. Wash-

ington, DC: The World Bank.
Derosiers, R., K. Kopf, and J. M. Yohe. 1978. Evaluation of AID Loan 489-T-088. Washington, DC: USAID.
Dore, Ronald. 1982. "Groups and Individuals." Pp. 13-27 in *Society in Transition with special reference to Korea*, edited by Yunshik Chang, Tai-Hwan Kwon, and Peter J. Donaldson. Seoul: Seoul National University Press.
Eberhard, Wolfram. 1968. "Problems of Historical Sociology." Pp. 16-28 in *State and Society*, edited by Reinhard Bendix, et al. Berkeley: University of California Press.
Evans, Peter B. 1979. *Dependent Development*. Baltimore: The Johns Hopkins University Press.
Evans, Peter B., and Dietrich Rueschemeyer. 1985. "The State and Economic Transformation: Toward an Analysis of the Conditions Underlying Effective Intervention." Pp. 44-77 in Peter B. Evans, Dietrich Rueschemeyer, and Theda Skocpol, eds. *Bringing the State Back In*. Cambridge: Cambridge University Press.
Evans, Peter B., Dietrich Rueschemeyer, and Theda Skocpol, eds. 1985. *Bringing the State Back In*. Cambridge: Cambridge University Press.
Evans, Peter B., Dietrich Rueschemeyer, and Evelyne H. Stephens, eds. 1985. *States versus Markets in the World-System*. Beverly Hills, CA: Sage Publications.
Evenson, Robert E. 1978. A Century of Productivity in U.S. Agriculture: An Analysis of the Role of Invention, Research, and Extension. Center Discussion Paper No. 293. New Haven, CT: Yale University, Economic Growth Center.
Evenson, Robert E., and Hans P. Binswanger. 1978. "Technology Transfer and Research Resource Allocation." Pp. 164-211 in *Induced Innovation*, edited by Hans P. Binswanger and Vernon W. Ruttan. Baltimore: The Johns Hopkins University Press.
Evenson, Robert E., and Yoav Kislev. 1975. *Agricultural Research and Productivity*. New Haven, CT: Yale University Press.
Evenson, Robert E., Paul E. Waggoner, and Vernon W. Ruttan. 1979. "Economic Benefits from Research: An Example from Agriculture." *Science* 205:1101-1107.
Feinberg, Richard E. 1983. *The Intemperate Zone: The Third World Challenge to U.S. Foreign Policy*. New York: W. W. Norton and Company.

Gerschenkron, Alexander. 1962. *Economic Backwardness in Historical Perspective: A Book of Essays.* Cambridge, MA: Harvard University Press.
Giddens, Anthony. 1985. *The Nation-State and Violence.* Berkeley: University of California Press.
Gilpin, Robert. 1987. *The Political Economy of International Economic Relations.* Princeton, NJ: Princeton University Press.
Gold, Thomas B. 1986. *State and Society in the Taiwan Miracle.* New York: M. E. Sharpe, Inc.
Goldman, Marshall I. 1983. *The U.S.S.R. in Crisis: The Failure of an Economic System.* New York: W. W. Norton and Company.
Gouldner, Alvin. 1979. *The Intellectuals and the Rise of the New Class.* New York: The Seabury Press.
Grabowski, Richard. 1982. "Peasantry, Technical Change, and Rural Poverty." *Peasant Studies* 9:197-204.
Grajdanzev, Andrew. 1944. *Modern Korea.* New York: Institute of Pacific Affairs.
Grindle, Merilee S. 1986. *State and Countryside: Development Policy and Agrarian Politics in Latin America.* Baltimore: The Johns Hopkins University Press.
Haggard, Stephan, and Chung-in Moon. 1983. "The South Korean State in the International Economy: Liberal, Dependent, or Mercantile?" Pp. 131-189 in *The Antinomies of Interdependence,* edited by John Gerard Ruggie. New York: Columbia University Press.
Hagstom, Warren. 1965. *The Scientific Community.* New York: Basic Books, Inc.
Hamilton, Clive. 1986. *Capitalist Industrialization in Korea.* Boulder, CO: Westview Press.
Hayami, Yujiro and Vernon W. Ruttan. 1985, 2d edition; 1971. *Agricultural Development: An International Perspective.* Baltimore: The Johns Hopkins University Press.
Hayami, Yujiro, Vernon W. Ruttan, and Herman M. Southworth, eds. 1979. *Agricultural Growth in Japan, Taiwan, Korea, and the Philippines.* Honolulu: The University Press of Hawaii.
Hayami, Yujiro, and Saburo Yamada. 1975. "Agricultural Research Organization in Economic Development: A Review of the Japanese Experience." Pp. 224-249 in *Agriculture in Development Theory,* edited by Lloyd G. Reynolds. New Haven, CT: Yale University Press.

Henderson, Gregory. 1968. *The Politics of the Vortex.* Cambridge, MA: Harvard University Press.

Hirschman, Albert O. 1970. *Exit, Voice, and Loyalty.* Cambridge, MA: Harvard University Press.

Ho, Samuel P. S. 1982. "Economic Development and Rural Industry in South Korea and Taiwan." *World Development* 10:973-990.

Horowitz, Irving Louis. 1982. *Beyond Empire and Revolution: Militarization and Consolidation in the Third World.* New York: Oxford University Press.

Hyden, Goran. 1983. *No Shortcuts to Progress.* Berkeley: University of California Press.

Im, Hyug Baeg. 1987. "The Rise of Bureaucratic Authoritarianism in South Korea." *World Politics* 39:231-257.

Jacobs, Norman. 1985. *The Korean Road to Modernization and Development.* Chicago: University of Illinois Press.

Johnson, Chalmers. 1982. *MITI and the Japanese Miracle: The Growth of Industrial Policy, 1925-1975.* Stanford, CA: Stanford University Press.

Johnston, Bruce F., and Peter Kilby. 1975. *Agricultural and Structural Transformation: Economic Strategies in Late-Developing Countries.* New York: Oxford University Press.

Jones, Leroy P., and Il Sakong. 1980. *Government, Business, and Entrepreneurship in Economic Development: The Korean Case.* Cambridge, MA: Harvard University Press.

Judd, M. Ann, James K. Boyce, and Robert E. Evenson. 1983. Investing in Agricultural Supply. Discussion Paper No. 442. New Haven, CT: Yale University, Economic Growth Center.

_____. 1986. "Investing in Agricultural Supply: The Determinants of Agricultural Research and Extension Investment." *Economic Development and Cultural Change* 34:77-113.

KASS. 1972. *Korean Agricultural Sector Study.* East Lansing: Michigan State University.

Katzenstein, Peter J., ed. 1978. *Between Power and Plenty: Foreign Economic Policies of Advanced Industrial States.* Madison: The University of Wisconsin Press.

_____. 1985. *Small States in World Markets.* Ithaca, NY: Cornell University Press.

Keidel, Albert. 1981. *Korean Regional Farm Product and Income: 1910-1975.* Seoul: Korea Development Institute.

Kerr, George H. 1965. *Formosa Betrayed.* Boston: Houghton Mifflin.

Kihl, Young Hwan. 1979. "Politics and Agrarian Change in South Korea: Rural Modernization by 'Induced' Mobilization." Pp. 133-169 in *Food, Politics, and Agricultural Development,* edited by Raymond F. Hopkins, Donald Pucchala, and Ross Talbot. Boulder, CO: Westview Press.

_____. 1984. *Politics and Policies in Divided Korea: Regimes in Contest.* Boulder, CO: Westview Press.

Kihl, Young Hwan, and Dong Suh Bark. 1981. "Food Policies in a Rapidly Developing Country: The Case of South Korea, 1960-1978." *The Journal of Developing Areas* 16:47-70.

Kim, Bun Woong, David S. Bell, Jr., and Chong Bum Lee, eds. 1985. *Administrative Dynamics and Development: The Korean Experience.* Seoul: Kyobo Publishing, Inc.

Kim, C. I. Eugene. 1984. "Civil-Military Relations in the Two Koreas." *Armed Forces and Society* 11:9-31.

Kim, Dong-Hi, and Yong-Jae Joo. 1982. *The Food Situation and Policies in the Republic of Korea.* Paris: OECD.

Kim, In Hwan. 1979. *The Green Revolution in Korea.* Suweon, Korea: Office of Rural Development.

Kim, Jai-Hyup. 1978. *The Garrison State in Pre-War Japan and Post-War Korea: A Comparative Analysis of Military Politics.* Washington, DC: University Press of America.

Kim, Ki-Hwan. 1980. *The Korean Economy: Current Reforms and Future Prospects.* Economic Bulletin No. 80-29.

Kim, Se-Jin. 1971. *The Politics of Military Revolution in Korea.* Chapel Hill: University of North Carolina Press.

Koo, Hagen. 1984. "World System, Class, and State in Third World Development: Toward an Integrative Framework of Political Economy." *Sociological Perspectives* 27:33-52.

Kornhauser, William. 1962. *Scientists in Industry: Conflict and Accommodation.* Berkeley: University of California Press.

Krasner, Stephen D. 1978. *Defending the National Interest: Raw Materials Investment and U.S. Foreign Policy.* Princeton, NJ: Princeton University Press.

_____. 1985. *Structural Conflict: The Third World Against Global Liberalism.* Berkeley: University of California Press.

Krishna, Raj. 1982. "Some Aspects of Agricultural Growth,

Price Policy and Equity in Developing Countries." *Food Research Institute Studies* 18:219-260.
Krueger, Anne O. 1983. "Effects of Trade Strategies on Growth." *Finance and Development* 20:6-8.
Kuo, Shirley W. Y., Gustav Ranis, and John C. H. Fei. 1981. *The Taiwan Success Story: Rapid Growth with Improved Distribution in the Republic of China, 1952-1979*. Boulder, CO: Westview Press.
Kwon, Hyunjoo P. 1974. *The Emergence of the Military Man in Korean Politics: A Historical Study of the Rise of Military Elites*. Buffalo, NY: SUNY-Buffalo.
Lee, Eddy. 1979. "Egalitarian Peasant Farming and Rural Development: The Case of South Korea." Pp. 24-71 in *Agrarian Systems and Rural Development*, edited by Daram Ghai, Azizur Rahman Khan, Eddy Lee, and Samir Radwan. New York: Holmes and Meier Publishers, Inc.
Lee, Hahn-Been. 1968. *Time, Change, and Administration*. Honolulu: East-West Center Press.
Lee, Man-Gap, ed. 1981. *Toward a New Community Life*. Seoul: Seoul National University, Institute of *Saemaul Undong* Studies.
Leipziger, D. M. and others. 1987. *Korea: Managing the Industrial Transition*. Washington, DC: The World Bank.
Lim, Hyun-Chin. 1985. *Dependent Development in Korea, 1963-1979*. Seoul: Seoul National University Press.
List, Friedrich. 1916 [1844]. *The National System of Political Economy*, translated by Sampson S. Lloyd. London: Longmans, Green.
Lockwood, William W. 1954. *The Economic Development of Japan: Growth and Structural Change, 1868-1938*. Princeton, NJ: Princeton University Press.
Lowi, Theodore J. 1979. *The End of Liberalism: The Second Republic of the United States*. New York: W. W. Norton and Company.
Luedde-Neurath, Richard. 1986. *Import Controls and Export-Oriented Development: A Reassessment of the South Korean Case*. Boulder, CO: Westview Press.
Malloy, James M. 1987. "The Politics of Transition in Latin America." Pp. 235-257 in *Authoritarians and Democrats: Regime Transition in Latin America*, edited by James M. Malloy and Mitchell A. Seligson. Pittsburgh, PA: University of Pittsburgh Press.
Martin, Michael V., and John A. McDonald. 1986. "Food

Grain Policy in the Republic of Korea: The Economic Costs of Self-Sufficiency." *Economic Development and Cultural Change* 34:315-331.
Matray, James I. 1985. *The Reluctant Crusade.* Honolulu: University of Hawaii Press.
McConnell, Grant. 1953. *The Decline of Agrarian Democracy.* Berkeley: University of California Press.
Merrill, John. 1983. "Internal Warfare in Korea, 1948-1950: The Local Setting of the Korean War." Pp. 133-162 in *Child of Conflict: The Korean-American Relationship, 1943-1953*, edited by Bruce Cumings. Seattle: University of Washington Press.
Merton, Robert K. 1973. *The Sociology of Science: Theoretical and Empirical Investigations.* Chicago: The University of Chicago Press.
Meyer, John W. 1981. "The World Polity and the Authority of the Nation-State." Pp. 109-137 in *Studies of the Modern World-System*, edited by Albert Bergesen. New York: Academic Press.
Michell, Tony. 1984. "Administrative Traditions and Economic Decision-Making in South Korea." Pp. 32-37 in *Developmental States in East Asia: Capitalist and Socialist*, edited by Robert Wade and Gordon White. IDS Bulletin No. 15. Sussex, England: Institute of Development Studies.
Migdal, Joel. 1985. "A Model of State-Society Relations." Pp. 41-55 in *New Directions in Comparative Politics*, edited by Howard J. Wiarda. Boulder, CO: Westview Press.
Ministry of Agriculture and Fisheries. 1962-1985. *Ministry of Agriculture and Fisheries Yearbooks.* Seoul: MAF.
Moon, Pal Yong. 1975. "The Evolution of Rice Policy in Korea." *Food Research Institute Studies* 14:381-401.
_____. 1984. "Agricultural Modernization and Rural Development." *Rural Review* 11:59-90.
Moore, Barrington. 1966. *Social Origins of Dictatorship and Democracy: Lord and Peasant in the Making of the Modern World.* Boston: Beacon Press.
Moore, Mick. 1984. "Agriculture in Taiwan and South Korea: The Minimalist State?" Pp. 57-64 in *Developmental States in East Asia: Capitalist and Socialist*, edited by Robert Wade and Gordon White. IDS Bulletin No. 15. Sussex, England: Institute of Development Studies.
_____. 1985. "Mobilization and Disillusion in Rural Korea: The Saemaul Movement in Retrospect." *Pacific*

Affairs 57:487-508.
Moskowitz, Paul. 1982. "Korean Development and Korean Studies—A Review." *Journal of Asian Studies* 42:63-90.
Mueller, Dennis C. 1979. *Public Choice*. New York: Cambridge University Press.
Mulkay, Michael. 1979. *Science and the Sociology of Knowledge*. London: George Allen and Unwin.
Myers, Ramon H., and Yamada Saburo. 1984. "Agricultural Development in the Empire." Pp. 420-452 in *The Japanese Colonial Empire*, edited by Mark R. Peattie and Ramon H. Myers. Seattle: University of Washington Press.
National Agricultural Cooperatives Federation. 1962-1986. *National Agricultural Cooperatives Federation Yearbooks*. Seoul: NACF.
Newfarmer, Richard S. 1983. "Multinationals and Marketplace Magic in the 1980s." Pp. 162-197 in *Multinational Corporations in the 1980s*, edited by C. Kindleberger and D. Andretsch. Cambridge, MA: MIT Press.
O'Connor, James. 1973. *The Fiscal Crisis of the State*. New York: St. Martin's Press.
OECD. 1979. *The Impact of the Newly Industrializing Countries on Production and Trade in Manufactures*. Paris: OECD.
Office of Rural Development. 1962-1985. *Office of Rural Development Research Reports* (in Korean). Suweon, Korea: ORD.
_____. 1962-1981. *Office of Rural Development Yearbooks*. Suweon, Korea: ORD.
Ogura, Takekazu. 1963. "The Meiji Restoration and Agriculture." Pp. 3-26 in *Agricultural Development in Modern Japan*, edited by Takekazu Ogura. Tokyo: Fuji Publishing Company, Ltd.
Olson, Mancur. 1965. *The Logic of Collective Action*. Cambridge, MA: Harvard University Press.
Oshima, Harry T. 1986. "The Transition from an Agricultural to an Industrial Economy in East Asia." *Economic Development and Cultural Change* 34:783-809.
Owen, Wyn F. 1966. "The Double Development Squeeze on Agriculture." *American Economic Review* 56:43-70.
Palais, James B. 1975. *Politics and Policy in Traditional Korea*. Cambridge, MA: Harvard University Press.
Park, Jin Hwan. 1981. "Process of *Saemaul Undong* Implementation in Korea." Pp. 133-159 in *Toward a New Com-*

munity, edited by Man-Gap Lee. Seoul: Seoul National University, Institute of *Saemaul Undong* Studies.
Park, Jung Keun. 1986. Technological Change in the Korean Rice Economy: Sources, Direction and Impact. Unpublished Ph.D. dissertation, University of Minnesota.
Pelz, Donald C., and Frank M. Andrews. 1976. *Scientists in Organizations: Productive Climates for Research and Development.* Ann Arbor, MI: Institute for Social Research.
Pineiro, Martin, and Edwardo Trigo. 1983. *Technical Change and Social Conflict in Agriculture: Latin American Perspectives.* Boulder, CO: Westview Press.
Polanyi, Karl. 1957. *The Great Transformation.* Boston: Beacon Press.
Pye, Lucien W. 1985. *Asian Power and Politics.* Cambridge, MA: Harvard University Press.
Ranis, Gustav. 1970. "The Financing of Japanese Economic Development." Pp. 37-57 in *Agriculture and Economic Growth: Japan's Experience*, edited by Kazushi Ohkawa, Bruce F. Johnston and Hiromatsu Kaneda. Princeton, NJ: Princeton University Press.
Reed, Edward P. 1979. Group Farming in South Korea. Unpublished Ph.D. dissertation, University of Wisconsin.
Rueschemeyer, Dietrich. 1986. *Power and the Division of Labor.* Stanford, CA: Stanford University Press.
Ruggie, John Gerard. 1983a. "International Regimes, Transactions, and Change: Embedded Liberalism in the Postwar Order." Pp. 195-231 in *International Regimes*, edited by Stephen D. Krasner. Ithaca, NY: Cornell University Press.
_____. 1983b. "Continuity and Transformation in the World Polity: Toward a Neorealist Synthesis." *World Politics* 35:261-285.
_____, ed. 1983c. *The Antinomies of Interdependence.* New York: Columbia University Press.
Ruttan, Vernon W. 1975. "Technological Transfer, Institutional Transfer, and Induced Technical and Institutional Change in Agricultural Development." Pp. 165-191 in *Agriculture in Development Theory*, edited by Lloyd G. Reynolds. New Haven, CT: Yale University Press.
_____. 1981. "Three Cases of Induced Institutional Innovation." Pp. 239-270 in *Public Choice and Rural Development*, edited by Clifford S. Russell and Norman K. Nicholson. Washington, DC: Resources for the Future,

Inc.
_____. 1982. *Agricultural Research Policy*. Minneapolis: University of Minnesota Press.
_____. 1983. Reforming the Global Agricultural Research Support System. Minneapolis: University of Minnesota, Economic Development Center.
Sanders, John H., and Vernon W. Ruttan. 1978. "Biased Choice of Technology in Brazilian Agriculture." Pp. 276-296 in *Induced Innovation*, edited by Hans P. Binswanger and Vernon W. Ruttan. Baltimore: The Johns Hopkins University Press.
Sawada, Shujiro. 1965. "Innovation in Japanese Agriculture, 1880-1935." Pp. 325-351 in *The State and Economic Enterprise in Japan*, edited by William W. Lockwood. Princeton, NJ: Princeton University Press.
Scitovsky, Tibor. 1985. "Economic Development in Taiwan and South Korea, 1965-1981." *Food Research Institute Studies* 19:215-264.
Shim, Young-Kun, and Brian Lockwood. 1976. "Strategies for Expanding Rice Production through Providing a Market." *Korean Journal of Agricultural Economics* 18:53-63.
Skocpol, Theda. 1979. *States and Revolutions*. New York: Cambridge University Press.
Steinberg, David I. 1985. Foreign Aid and the Development of the Republic of Korea: The Effectiveness of Concessional Assistance. AID Evaluation Special Study No. 42. Washington, DC: USAID.
Steinberg, David I., Sung Hwan Ban, W. Donald Bowles, and Maureen A. Lewis. 1984. Korean Agricultural Services: The Invisible Hand in the Iron Glove. Market and Nonmarket Forces in Korean Rural Development. AID Project Evaluation Report No. 52. Washington, DC: USAID.
Steiner, Peter O. 1977. "The Public Sector and the Public Interest." Pp. 27-66 in *Public Expenditure and Policy Analysis*, edited by Robert H. Haveman and Julius Margolis. Chicago: Rand McNally College Publishing Company.
Stepan, Alfred. 1978. *The State and Society: Peru in Comparative Perspective*. Princeton, NJ: Princeton University Press.
Timmer, C. Peter. 1986. *Getting the Prices Right: The Scope and Limits of Agricultural Price Policy*. Ithaca, NY:

Cornell University Press.
Thomas, Clive Y. 1984. *The Rise of the Authoritarian State in Peripheral Societies.* New York: Monthly Review Press.
Wade, Robert. 1982. *Irrigation and Agricultural Politics in South Korea.* Boulder, CO: Westview Press.
_____. 1983. "South Korea's Agricultural Development: The Myth of the Passive State." *Pacific Viewpoint* 24:11-28.
Wade, Robert, and Gordon White, eds. 1984. *Developmental States in East Asia: Capitalist and Socialist.* IDS Bulletin No. 15. Sussex, England: Institute of Development Studies.
Waltz, Kenneth N. 1979. *Theory of International Politics.* Reading, MA: Addison-Wesley Publishing Company.
Wolf, Eric R. 1969. *Peasant Wars of the Twentieth Century.* New York: Harper and Row, Publishers.
Wood, Robert E. 1986. *From Marshall Plan to Debt Crisis: Foreign Aid and Development Choices in the World Economy.* Berkeley: University of California Press.
World Bank. *World Development Report 1986.* Washington, DC: The World Bank.
Zysman, John. 1983. *Governments, Markets, and Growth.* Ithaca, NY: Cornell University Press.

Subject Index

Agrarian problem, 151
Agricultural Association Law (Japan), 24
Agricultural commodity demand, in Korea, 84, 85(table)
Agricultural commodity supply, in Korea, 84-85, 86(table)
Agricultural development
  in Northeast Asia, 5
  in Latin America, 157-158
Agricultural Development Corporation, 131
Agricultural growth rates
  in Korea, 1, 3, 4
  in newly industrializing countries (NICs), 4
Agricultural policy, in Korea, 5
  history of, 10n.3
Agricultural price policy, in Korea, 10n.3, 66, 67(table), 68, 92
Agricultural protectionism, in Northeast Asia, 4
Agricultural research
  commodity congruity index, 76-77, 81-82(tables)
  consumer orientation of, 99
  crop variety releases, in Korea, 87-88(table)
  decentralized systems of, 105, 126
  deconcentrated systems of, 106, 126
  horticultural crops, characteristics of, 83-84
  in Japan, 22-24
  in Latin America, 158-160
  livestock, characteristics of, 83
  marketing, in Korea, 96
  parity allocation model of, 76-80(table)
  policies. *See* Induced innovation; Directed innovation.
    in Korea, 6
    in NICs, 151
  publications, in Korea, 90-91(table)
  public goods, characteristics of, 17-18
  in U.S., 20-22
American Farm Bureau Federation, 20, 21
Argentina, politics in, 158
Authority in organizations, definition of, 102

Barley, 88-89, 93

Brandt, Willy, 31
Brazil, agricultural research investments in, 161
  economic growth and politics in, 150
  politics in, 158
Bureaucratic-authoritarian (BA) regimes, 15, 104, 150, 151, 152, 165
  in Latin America, 156-157, 166, 167
  in Northeast Asia, 150, 156-157

CABA. See Commonwealth Agricultural Bureau Abstracts.
Cardenas, Lazaro, 163
Central ORD institutes, 104, 122-123
  researchers in, social background characteristics of, 106
Chang, Myon, 40
Chiang, Kai-shek, 153
Chile, agricultural research investments in, 161
  politics in, 158
China, Civil War in, 153
  Manchu dynasty in, 48
  relations with precolonial Korea, 47
  socialist autarky in, 15, 27
  U.S. recognition of, 71
  war with Japan, 33
Chun, Doo Hwan, 63, 74n.6, 164
CIA (Korean), 70, 74n.6, 164
Class structure
  in postcolonial Korea, 39-40, 42, 68, 172
  in Yi dynasty Korea, 47-48. *See Yangban.*
Colombia, agricultural research investment in, 161
  politics in, 158
Commonwealth Agricultural Bureau Abstracts, 91.
Communist party, in Korea, 32, 36
Competitive advantage, 3, 10n.2
Confucianism, 48, 128
CORD. *See* Central ORD institutes.
Crop acreages, in Korea, 84-85(table)
Cropping systems, in Korea, 57-58, 74n.5, 90
Cuba, socialist revolution in, 167

Dependent development, 151
Development, definition of, 7
Developmental state, 15-17

Directed innovation, 26-29
  political economy assumptions of, 28-29

Economic Planning Board, 43, 127, 129, 131
Embedded liberalism, 166
EPB. *See* Economic Planning Board.
Extension. *See* Rural Guidance Office.

Farmers' associations (FAs), in Taiwan, 153, 154, 164

Germany, division of, 31
Greater East Asian Co-Prosperity Sphere, 93
Greece, NIC status of, 10n.4

Homogeneity, in Korean agriculture, 80-81. *See* Unimodal agrarian structure.
Hong Kong, city-state characteristics of, 151
  NIC status of, 10n.4
Horticultural crops, 71, 89, 92, 95-96

Illicit Wealth Accumulation Law, 42
Import substitution
  agricultural, 3, 69-70, 90, 94, 158
  industrial, 157, 168
India, agricultural production in, 80
Indonesia, agricultural production in, 80
Induced innovation, 6-7, 101-102
  class efficiency variant of, 25, 159-160
  impure form of, 23-25
  political economy assumptions of, 27-28, 102
  pure form of, 18-19
Influence in organizations, definition of, 103
International Rice Research Institute, 51, 52, 53, 87-88
Intersectoral articulation, definition of, 14
IRRI. *See* International Rice Research Institute.
Italy, latecomer development in, 14

Japan, agricultural research in, history of, 22-24
  colonial policies of, 32-35, 50, 87, 93, 129, 154
  latecomer development in, 14
  relations with precolonial Korea, 49
  Meiji Restoration in, 22-24
  Tokugawa period in, 22-23

world system position of, 33
Joint Committee on Rural Reconstruction (JCRR), in Taiwan, 153, 154
Joint farming strategies, in Korea, 59

KASS, 56, 70, 85(table)
Kim, Dae-Jung, 70
Kim, Il Sung, 31, 32
Kim, In Hwan, 52, 55, 56, 59, 60
Knapp, Seaman, 20
Korean Agricultural Sector Study. *See* KASS.
Korean Democratic People's Republic, in North Korea, 32
Korean People's Republic, 36-37
Korean War, 35
KPR. *See* Korean People's Republic.
Kuomintang (KMT), in Taiwan, 154, 156, 164-165

Land reform, 44
  by Korean People's Republic, 36, 38
  in Meiji Japan, 23
  in Mexico, 163
  in North Korea, 38
  in South Korea, 38-39, 44-45, 46
  in Taiwan, 44-45
Latin America, 15, 166. *See individual countries.*
  agrarian structure in, 158, 160-161, 163
  class structure in, 156
  social disarticulation in, 25, 46, 160-161
Livestock, 71, 85-86(table), 89-90, 92

MAF. *See* Ministry of Agriculture and Fisheries.
Malaysia, agricultural production in, 79
  agricultural research in, 77
Manchuria, Japanese colonial annexation of, 33
Marx, Karl, 25, 47, 157
Mexico, agricultural research investment in, 161
  land reform in, 163
  politics in, 158, 164, 165
  revolution in, 163
MHA. *See* Ministry of Home Affairs.
Military sector
  in Korea, 31, 40-41, 43, 47
    1961 coup, 41-42, 71

    personnel, social background characteristics of, 41-42, 170
  in Latin America, 167
  in Taiwan, 169
  as world system component, 16-17
Ministry of Agriculture and Fisheries, 55, 60, 63, 127, 131
Ministry of Commerce and Industry, 129, 130, 131
Ministry of Construction, 131
Ministry of Finance (Japan), 129
Ministry of Home Affairs, 43, 45, 130
Ministry of International Trade and Industry (Japan), 129
Monroe Doctrine, 167

National Agricultural Cooperatives Federation (NACF), 45-46, 131
New Community Movement (NCM), 45-46, 66
Newly industrializing countries (NICs)
  agricultural research policies in, 150
  bureaucratic-authoritarian politics in, 150-151
  definition of, 10n.4
  developmental state in, 15-17
  economic history of, 4, 14-15
  location within world system, 15-16
  military sector in, 15-17
Nigeria, agricultural production in, 79
North Korean Workers' Party (NKWP), 31, 32, 37
North-South competition, in Korea, 42-43, 62, 72
North-South division, of Korea, 31, 35, 47

Office of Rural Development (ORD), establishment of, 44
Organization theory, 98
  population ecology model, 99
Oriental despotism, 47

Pakistan, agricultural production in, 80
Park, Chung-Hee, 41, 42, 43, 52, 54, 62, 70, 74n.6, 130, 164, 170
Patrimonialism, 130-131
People's committees, 36, 38
Peru, agricultural research investment in, 161
  politics in, 158, 168
Philippines, agricultural production in, 79
Political economy, definition of, 6, 11n.6

Political parties
 in Korea, 164
 in Latin America, 163-164
 in Taiwan, 164-165. See Kuomintang.
PORD. See Provincial ORD institutes.
Portugal, NIC status of, 10n.4
Provincial ORD institutes, 105, 122-123
 researchers in, social background characteristics of, 106
Prussia, latecomer development in, 14
Public Law (PL) 480 (U.S.), 68-69, 94. See United States bilateral assistance, to Korea.

Realpolitik, 172
 definition of, 4
Red peasant unions, 35
Republic of Korea (South Korea), establishment of, 38
Research intensity, 82-84(tables)
RGO. See Rural guidance office.
Rhee, Syngman, 37-38, 39, 40, 170
Rice blast, 62-63
Rice marketing, in Korea, 56-57, 66, 68(table)
Rice varieties
 acreage of, in Korea, 61(table)
 indica type of, 53, 73n.2, 73-74n.4
 IR-8, 51, 53
 japonica type of, 51, 73n.2
 regional distribution of, in Korea, 50
 Tongil type of, 53, 62(table)
Rural Development Administration, 44
Rural guidance office, 58-59, 63, 111, 114-115
Russia, latecomer development in, 14
 relations with precolonial Korea, 49
 war with Japan, 33

Saemaul Undong. See New Community Movement.
Science, sociology of, 98, 99-101, 117-118
Scientific professionalization, 118
Scientist-administrator role, 107, 110
Singapore
 city-state characteristics of, 151
 NIC status of, 10n.4
Sino-Japanese War, 48
Smith-Lever Act (U.S.), 20

Social articulation, in Korean agriculture, 46
Social disarticulation, in Latin American agriculture, 25, 160-161.
Soviet Union, involvement in Korea, 32, 35, 37
Spain, NIC status of, 10n.4
Sri Lanka, agricultural production in, 79
State autonomy, 16, 25, 26, 103-104
   in Korea, 31, 42, 71, 169-170, 172
   in Latin America, 157, 160, 166-167, 168
   in Taiwan, 169, 172
State/society relationship, 14-15, 16, 19, 29n.1, 162
   as exclusionary statism, 26, 42, 103
   as inclusionary corporatism, 26, 29n.3
   in Korea, 73, 127-128
   in Taiwan, 156
Status differentials, in Korea, 116, 121, 132

Taiwan, agrarian structure in, 154, 164
   class structure in, 172
   economic development in, 152
   economics and politics in, 150
   intersectoral articulation in, 152
   Japanese colonial rule in, 33-34
   Kuomintang in, 164-165
Thailand, agricultural production in, 80
Transnational corporations (TNCs), 15, 166, 167
Trusteeship, Korean peninsula, 35
"2-28 Incident" (Taiwan), 156

Unimodal agrarian structure, 39, 80-81, 155, 162
United States, agricultural development in, 151
   agricultural research in, history of, 20-22
   bilateral assistance
     to Korea, 51, 68-69, 73n.3, 89, 170
     to Taiwan (and China), 153, 170
   policy
     toward Asia, 71
     toward Korea, 35-38, 69
     toward Latin America, 167
United States Agency for International Development (USAID), 89, 154
Uruguay, politics in, 158

Venezuela, agricultural research investment in, 161
   politics in, 158
Vietnam, division of, 31

Weber, Max, 30
Wheat, 88-89, 93-95
Wilson, Woodrow, 171
Wittfogel, Karl, 47
World Bank study, of Korea, 3
World system, 12-17
   associative articulation strategies in, 15
   economic dimension of, 14
   interstate dimension of, 12-14
   peripheral societies in, 16
   science in, 101
   semiperipheral societies in, 10n.4. *See* Newly industrializing countries.
   theoretical issues in, 165-167, 170-171
   warfare/welfare imperative in, 13
World time, 32, 166

Yangban class, 47
Yi dynasty Korea, 31, 47
Yi, Ha-Eung (*Taewongun*), 48
Yoe, Un-Hyeong, 35
Yugoslavia, NIC status of, 10n.4

Author Index

Adelman, Irma, 70
Alavi, Hamza, 16
Aldrich, Howard, 98, 99
Amsden, Alice, 155, 156
Anderson, Kym, 4
Andrews, Frank M., 99
Apthorpe, Raymond, 44, 154
Aqua, Ronald, 43, 59, 135

Bacharach, Samuel, 103
Ban, Sung Hwan, 1, 3, 4, 10n.3, 45, 66, 70, 131
Bank of Korea, 2
Bark, Dong Suh, 10
Barker, Randolph, 73n.2
Barone, Charles A., 46
Beachell, H. M., 61
Bell, Daniel, 101
Bell, David S., Jr., 132
Bendix, Reinhard, 12, 14
Berry, R. A., 80
Binswanger, Hans P., 6, 19, 101
Bowles, W. Donald, 45
Boyce, James K., 76, 77, 78, 79, 82, 84, 90, 92
Brandt, Vincent S. R., 66
Browett, John, 10n.4
Burmeister, Larry L., 5, 7, 8, 13, 26, 66, 67, 84, 97n.1, 129
Busch, Lawrence, 90, 98, 100, 102, 104
Buzan, Barry, 29n.1

Cardoso, Fernando Henrique, 49n.1
Carnoy, Martin, 25
Chalmers, Douglas A., 29n.1
Chen, Ching-chih, 33
Cho, Chang Hyun, 43
Clough, Ralph N., 153
Cole, David C., 41, 42, 69
Cole, Jonathan R., 100
Cole, Stephen, 100
Collier, David, 15, 151, 157
Collins, Randall, 12, 29n.1, 30

Crane, Diana, 100
Crill, Pat, 61
Cumings, Bruce, 7, 32, 35, 36, 38, 152, 154, 170

Dahl, Robert A., 66
Dalrymple, Dana G., 61, 62, 63, 64
Danbom, Charles, 21
de Janvry, Alain, 7, 25, 44, 46, 159, 160, 161, 163
Derosiers, R., 74n.5, 94
Dethier, Jean Jacques, 7, 25, 159, 160, 161
Dore, Ronald, 128

Eberhard, Wolfram, 166
Evans, Peter B., 7, 16, 151, 167
Evenson, Robert E., 66, 76, 77, 78, 79, 82, 83, 84, 90, 91, 92, 101, 102

Faletto, Enzo, 49n.1
Fei, John C. H., 152, 155
Feinberg, Richard E., 14, 28

Gerschenkron, Alexander, 12, 14
Giddens, Anthony, 12, 29n.1, 166
Gilpin, Robert, 11n.6
Gold, Thomas B., 156
Goldman, Marshall, 15
Gouldner, Alvin, 101
Grabowski, Richard, 7
Grajdanzev, Andrew, 34, 38
Grindle, Merilee S., 158, 159, 163, 168

Haggard, Stephan, 7
Hagstrom, Warren, 100
Ham, Y. S., 61
Hamilton, Clive, 4, 7
Hayami, Yujiro, 1, 6, 19, 22, 24, 34, 87, 101
Henderson, Gregory, 36, 40, 48
Herdt, Robert W., 73n.2
Hirschman, Albert O., 128
Ho, Samuel P. S., 8
Horowitz, Irving Louis, 12, 16, 17, 167
Hyden, Goran, 46

Im, Hyug Baeg, 15, 151

Jacobs, Norman, 105, 130
Johnson, Chalmers, 16, 22, 25, 129
Johnston, Bruce F., 39, 80, 152
Jones, Leroy P., 7, 40, 66, 104
Joo, Yong-Jae, 10n.3, 67, 70, 85, 161
Judd, M. Ann, 77, 78, 79, 82, 83, 84, 90, 92

KASS, 56, 70, 85
Katzenstein, Peter J., 7, 16, 29n.1
Keidel, Albert, 71
Kerr, George H., 156
Kihl, Young Hwan, 7, 10n.3, 31, 32, 45, 47, 62, 170
Kilby, Peter, 39, 80, 152
Kim, Bun Woong, 128, 132
Kim, C. I. Eugene, 31
Kim, Dong-Hi, 10n.3, 67, 70, 85, 161
Kim, In Hwan, 50, 51, 52, 53, 54, 55, 56, 59, 60, 73n.1, 87
Kim, Jai-Hyup, 71
Kim, Ki-Hwan, 72
Kim, Se-Jin, 40
Kislev, Yoav, 90
Koo, Hagen, 15, 165
Kopf, K., 74n.5, 94
Kornhauser, William, 99
Krasner, Stephen D., 27, 28, 171
Krishna, Raj, 1, 4
Krueger, Anne O., 3
Kuo, Shirley W. Y., 152, 155
Kwon, Hyunjoo P., 40

Lacy, William B., 90, 98, 100, 102, 104
Lawler, Edward J., 103
Lee, Chong Bum, 132
Lee, Eddy, 70
Lee, Hahn-Been, 42, 43
Lee, Man-Gap, 66
Leipziger, D. M., 3
Lewis, Maureen A., 45
Lim, Hyun-Chin, 15, 151
Lindblom, Charles E., 66
List, Friedrich, 7

Lockwood, Brian, 29n.1
Lockwood, William W., 56
Lowi, Theodore J., 21
Luedde-Neurath, Richard, 3, 7
Lyman, Princeton N., 41, 42

Malloy, James M., 157, 168
Martin, Michael V., 11n.7
Matray, James I., 32, 35, 36
McConnell, Grant, 20
McDonald, John A., 11n.7
Merrill, John, 38
Merton, Robert K., 99, 100
Meyer, John W., 16
Michell, Tony, 128, 129, 130, 131
Migdal, Joel, 29n.1, 162
Ministry of Agriculture and Fisheries, 61, 81, 82, 84, 86
Moon, Chung-in, 7
Moon, Pal Yong, 1, 2, 3, 10n.3, 11n.7, 66, 70
Moore, Barrington, 14
Moore, Mick, 45, 154, 156
Moskowitz, Paul, 40, 44
Mueller, Dennis C., 17
Mulkay, Michael, 100
Myers, Ramon H., 7

National Agricultural Cooperatives Federation, 57, 68
Newfarmer, Richard S., 14

O'Conner, James, 17
OECD, 10
Office of Rural Development, 81, 82, 84, 88, 92
Ogura, Takekazu, 23, 24, 29n.1
Olson, Mancur, 4
Oshima, Harry T., 5, 152
Owen, Wyn F., 151

Palais, James B., 31, 47
Park, Jin Hwan, 66
Park, Jung Keun, 2, 97n.1
Park, Yung Chul, 69
Pelz, Donald C., 99
Perkins, Dwight H., 1, 3, 10n.3, 66, 70

Pineiro, Martin, 7, 159, 160
Polanyi, Karl, 14
Pye, Lucien W., 7, 129, 132

Ranis, Gustav, 23, 152, 155
Reed, Edward P., 59
Robinson, Sherman, 70
Rose, Beth, 73
Rueschemeyer, Dietrich, 7, 16, 118
Ruggie, John Gerard, 13, 14, 15, 166
Ruttan, Vernon W., 1, 6, 18, 19, 22, 24, 34, 66, 75, 76, 77, 78, 87, 101, 102, 105, 159

Saburo, Yamada, 7
Sachs, Carolyn, 104
Sakong, Il, 7, 40, 66, 104
Sanders, John H., 24, 159
Sawada, Shujiro, 23
Scitovsky, Tibor, 4, 152
Shim, Young-Kun, 56
Skocpol, Theda, 7, 22, 29n.1
Southworth, Herman M., 1
Steinberg, David I., 45, 73n.2, 129
Steiner, Peter O., 17
Stepan, Alfred., 14, 29n.1
Stephens, Evelyne Huber, 7

Thomas, Clive Y., 25
Timmer, C. Peter, 4
Trigo, Edwardo, 7, 159, 160

Wade, Robert, 7, 45, 55, 96
Waggoner, Paul E., 66, 102
Waltz, Kenneth N., 12
White, Gordon, 7
Wolf, Eric R., 163
Wood, Robert E., 3, 28
World Bank, 2

Yamada, Saburo, 22
Yohe, J. M., 74n.5, 94

Zysman, John, 10n.2, 28

DATE DUE

DEMCO 38-297